THE GUERNICA BULL

Pablo Picasso, *Minotauromachy*. 1935. Etching, 19½″ × 27⁷⁄₁₆″.
Collection, The Museum of Modern Art, New York. Purchase
Fund.

THE GUERNICA BULL

Studies in the Classical Tradition
in the Twentieth Century

Harry C. Rutledge

THE UNIVERSITY OF GEORGIA PRESS

ATHENS AND LONDON

© 1989 by the University of Georgia Press
Athens, Georgia 30602
All rights reserved
Designed by Betty McDaniel
Set in Optima Medium
The paper in this book meets the guidelines for
permanence and durability of the Committee on
Production Guidelines for Book Longevity of the
Council on Library Resources.

Printed in the United States of America

93 92 91 90 89   5 4 3 2 1

Library of Congress Cataloging in Publication Data
Rutledge, Harry C.
    The Guernica bull: studies in the classical tradition
in the twentieth century / Harry C. Rutledge.
        p. cm.
    Bibliography: p.
    Includes index.
    ISBN 0-8203-1064-6 (alk. paper)
    1. Literature, Modern—20th century—History and criticism.
2. Literature, Modern—20th century—Classical influences.
3. Classicism. I. Title.
PN771.R8 1989
809'.9142—dc19   88-5743
                                                          CIP
British Library Cataloging in Publication Data available.

For
FREDERICK NICKLAUS

Contents

Preface   ix

Acknowledgments   xi

Introduction   1

1 The Olympian World of Thomas Mann   10

2 The Resonant World of Pablo Picasso   22

3 Archetypal Hellas: The Theater of Cocteau, Gide,
   Giraudoux, Eliot   43

4 Art and Power: Hermann Broch's *The Death of Vergil*   63

5 Changing Visions: Three American Poets in Italy   74

6 Marguerite Yourcenar: The Classicism of *Feux* and
   Mémoires d'Hadrien   93

   Epilogue: Toward the End of the Century   112

   Notes   121

   Bibliography   141

   Index   151

Preface

A number of fellow scholars and old friends have, happily, been interested in this book.

The Mann chapter benefited from the reading by Edward Best, University of Georgia, and Phillip Rhein, Vanderbilt University. Throughout the writing of the book I have had the keen encouragement of Marija Petrovska, University of Tennessee, Knoxville. Eddie Harding, while a graduate student in the Department of Germanic and Slavic Languages, University of Tennessee, Knoxville, helped me greatly with Broch's commentaries on *Der Tod des Vergil*. I am grateful to the editors of *Classical and Modern Literature* for permission to reprint, with some adjustments, the study of Marguerite Yourcenar. To Bobbie Wayland Owenby great thanks for her several drafts of the book. Susan D. Martin, University of Tennessee, Knoxville, read and edited with the skill and judgment of both a classicist and a comparatist. The suggestions of the two referees were most useful.

The book had its beginning in lectures on Propertius by Kenneth M. Abbott, professor emeritus, Ohio State University, by whom I was introduced to Colin Wilson's *The Outsider*. Later I had the privilege of teaching with James W. Alexander, professor emeritus, University of Georgia, who showed me many harmonies between Past and Present. More recently, I have had the good advice of Kenneth Curry, professor emeritus, University of Tennessee, Knoxville. I am grateful to these scholars and connoisseurs.

There is a deep source almost beyond telling. The poet and friend to whom the book is dedicated remembers the old talk in the green room with its dormered windows, and mild summer nights on a trellised porch. His poems are at the heart of the book.

The faults and flaws of the book are completely my own responsibility.

Acknowledgments

The author and the publisher gratefully acknowledge permission to reprint excerpts from the following works.

Hermann Broch, *The Death of Vergil*, translated by Jean Starr Untermeyer (New York: Pantheon Books, 1945). Reprinted by permission of Pantheon Books, a division of Random House, Inc.

C. P. Cafavy, "Orophernes," from *The Complete Poems of Cafavy*, translated and copyright © 1961 by Rae Dalven. Reprinted by permission of Harcourt Brace Jovanovich, Inc.

Jean Cocteau, *Orpheus, Oedipus Rex, The Infernal Machine*, translated by Carl Wildman (London: Oxford University Press, 1962). Reprinted by permission of Oxford University Press.

James Dickey, "In the Lupanar at Pompeii." Copyright © 1961 by James Dickey. Reprinted from *Drowning with Others* by permission of Wesleyan University Press.

T. S. Eliot, *The Family Reunion*, copyright 1939 by T. S. Eliot; renewed 1967 by Esme Valerie Eliot. Reprinted by permission of Harcourt Brace Jovanovich, Inc.

T. S. Eliot, "Burnt Norton," "East Coker," and "Little Gidding," from *Four Quartets*, copyright 1943 by T. S. Eliot; renewed 1971 by Esme Valerie Eliot. Reprinted by permission of Harcourt Brace Jovanovich, Inc.

William Empson, "Doctrinal Point," from *Collected Poems of William Empson*, copyright 1949, 1977 by William Empson. Reprinted by permission of Harcourt Brace Jovanovich, Inc.

André Gide, *Two Legends: Oedipus and Theseus*, translated by John Russell (New York: Vintage Books, 1958). Reprinted by permission of Alfred A. Knopf, Inc.

Jean Giraudoux, *Tiger at the Gates*, translated by Christopher Fry (New York: Oxford University Press, 1955). Reprinted by permission of Oxford University Press.

Thomas Mann, *Stories of Three Decades*, translated by H. T. Lowe-Porter (New York: Alfred A. Knopf, 1936). Reprinted by permission of Alfred A. Knopf, Inc.

Frederick Nicklaus, *Cut of Noon* (New York: David Lewis, 1971). Reprinted by permission of Frederick Nicklaus.

Theodore Roethke, "The Far Field." Copyright © 1962 by Beatrice Roethke as administratrix of the estate of Theodore Roethke. From *The Collected Poems of Theodore Roethke*. Reprinted by permission of Doubleday, a division of Bantam, Doubleday, Dell Publishing Group, Inc.

Harry Rutledge, "Marguerite Yourcenar: The Classicism of *Feux* and *Mémoires d'Hadrien*," *Classical and Modern Literature* 4 (1984): 87–99. Reprinted by permission of CML, Inc.

W. D. Snodgrass, "The Operation," from *Heart's Needle* (New York: Alfred A. Knopf, 1959). Reprinted by permission of Alfred A. Knopf, Inc.

Trumbull Stickney, *The Poems of Trumbull Stickney*, edited by Amberys R. Whittle. Copyright © 1977, 1969, 1972 by Amberys R. Whittle. Reprinted by permission of Farrar, Straus and Giroux, Inc.

Richard Wilbur, "A Baroque Wall-Fountain in the Villa Sciarra," from *Things of This World*, copyright © 1956, 1984 by Richard Wilbur. Reprinted by permission of Harcourt Brace Jovanovich, Inc.

Tennessee Williams, *A Streetcar Named Desire*. Copyright 1947 by Tennessee Williams. Reprinted by permission of New Directions Publishing Corporation.

Marguerite Yourcenar, *Feux*. Copyright © 1984 by Editions Gallimard. Reprinted by permission of Editions Gallimard.

Marguerite Yourcenar, *Fires*. Translation copyright © 1981 by Dori Katz. Reprinted by permission of Farrar, Straus and Giroux, Inc.

Marguerite Yourcenar, *Mémoires d'Hadrien*. Copyright © 1974 by Editions Gallimard. Reprinted by permission of Editions Gallimard.

Marguerite Yourcenar, *Memoirs of Hadrian*. Copyright © 1963 by Marguerite Yourcenar. Reprinted by permission of Farrar, Straus and Giroux, Inc.

THE GUERNICA BULL

Introduction

Awake! Give thyself to the lovely hours.
Drinking their lips, catch thou the dream in flight
About their fragile hairs' aërial gold.
Thou art divine, thou livest, as of old
Apollo springing naked to the light,
And all his island shivered into flowers.
>   —Trumbull Stickney, "Live blindly
>   and upon the hour" (1898)

I've been on to you from the start! Not once did you pull any wool over
this boy's eyes! You come in here and sprinkle the place with powder and
spray perfume and cover the light-bulb with a paper lantern, and lo and
behold the place has turned into Egypt and you are the Queen of the Nile!
>   —Tennessee Williams, *A Streetcar Named Desire* (1947)

The achievements in the several arts by a great number of artists in the twentieth century make this era one of the greatest artistic periods in human history. Similar fecund eras that come to mind are Periclean Athens, Augustan Rome, the twelfth and thirteenth centuries, the age of Michelangelo, the reign of Louis XIV, and the reign of Queen Victoria.

The attainments and the standards of Athens and Rome produced the Western world's concept of classicism. The Parthenon, as well as the other buildings of the Periclean epoch, still seemed new in the time of Plutarch (writing in the late first century A.D.). In the Early Empire the commonality of Roman culture could only have impressed the traveler, as it does today. In Roman France the aqueducts and amphitheaters of Roman Italy, especially Augustan Italy, were copied everywhere, many of the monuments still surviving at such places as Arles and Nîmes. Then there is the admiration for the works of Vergil, whose *Aeneid* Augustus himself ordered to be promulgated after the death of the poet. Vergil's epic became standard reading upon its publication. Admiration for classicism pervaded the thinking of writers and artists of every art through the nineteenth century. For literature, there is a full survey of the many significant uses of the Antique in Gilbert Highet's *The Classical Tradition: Greek and Roman Influences on Western Literature* (1949). There is no such coverage, in English, for the other arts. Useful, however, are Walter Agard, *Classical Myths in Sculpture* (1951); Benjamin Rowland, *The Classical Tradition in Western Art* (1963); Cornelius Vermeule, *European Art and the Classical Past* (1964). These works have the same encyclopedic program for the plastic arts as does Highet's for literature. Rowland's book, however, although comprehensive in its catalog, is brief on each artist considered. Vermeule chose to end his survey with the first half of the nineteenth century. Recently, two rather differently conceived books have appeared which, because of their concentration and sharpness of focus, are more useful than the very broad works just cited. Of great interest is Francis Haskell and Nicholas Penny, *Taste and the Antique: The Lure of Classical Sculpture, 1500–1900* (1981). Richly informative and a model of its kind is Richard Jenkyns, *The Victorians and Ancient Greece* (1980), which has had considerable influence on the approach of the present work.

The essential concern of this book is the uses of classicism by several artists of the twentieth century. Although the choice of figures is highly selective, the range in time and in genre may provide a current description of "the present-day vitality of the classical tradition."[1] The book is not intended

at all to be a catalog; it is rather my hope to show the undula-
tions in our conception of the Classical during this century,
at least as far as the beginning of its final quarter. That is, the
uses of classical references by Thomas Mann in *Death in
Venice* (1912) are naturally closer to the formal and pictur-
esque appreciation of Trumbull Stickney's poem of 1898, the
last lines of which are part of the epigraph, than to the brilliant, fierce expressionism of Tennessee Williams, from
whose masterpiece, *A Streetcar Named Desire*, comes the
second epigraph. At the other end of the continuum, the
poetry of such writers as Frederick Nicklaus and James
Dickey shows classical influences in a less studied manner
but no less cogently than Stickney and Mann, and with the
powerful dramatic impact of such more recent borrowers
from the Antique as Tennessee Williams.[2]

As I have suggested elsewhere, I believe that at some
point, nearer the end of the century, the work of Gilbert
Highet should be brought up to date.[3] It is, after all, nearly
forty years since his great survey was published. But will it be
enough simply to survey the twentieth-century literature
that uses classical motifs? What is one to do with such masterpieces of the film as *Black Orpheus* (1959) and *Sundays
and Cybele* (1962)? How seriously should we take Jackson
Pollock's painting *Pasiphaë* (1943)? Surely such a survey
should deal with Stravinsky's oratorio *Oedipus Rex* (1927),
and possibly such music as Roger Sessions's *Idyll of The-
ocritus* (1956). The task would be tremendous, if one were to
cover all of the arts.

There is yet another problem, summed up in the term
modernism. Trumbull Stickney's poem is modern neither in
conception nor in diction, if we are to understand modernism as supported by and embracing the modes of expression

signified by the twentieth-century terms *Surrealism* and *Cubism.* There has been in this century a deliberate withdrawal from the centuries-old "cult of beauty," as in the case of Picasso's startling painting of 1907, *Les Demoiselles d'Avignon,* combined with a new conception of what is beautiful, as seen in such painterly examples as the work of Braque and Matisse.

The great feature of modern art is its quest for the expression of the deepest reality, eschewing all the while the Romanticism of the late eighteenth and early nineteenth centuries, the governing method being abstraction. To such painters as Picasso, Braque, and Matisse can be joined in spirit the following cluster of literary figures from 1922–23, the years immediately following the crest of the Cubist epoch: James Joyce (*Ulysses*), T. S. Eliot (*The Waste Land*), and Rainer Maria Rilke (*Duino Elegies*). J. B. Leishman's and Stephen Spender's summary of Rilke's "problem" can serve as a generalization:

> [The problem] was to find symbolic, or what he called "external," equivalents for experiences that were becoming even more "inward" and incommunicable, and which, when he tried to communicate them, were continually bringing him up against the limitations of language; our problem is to relate these symbols, these "external equivalents," to the experiences they symbolize, or (putting the matter less abstractly) to allow their incantation or suggestion to extend our normal consciousness until it is, for a moment, co-extensive with his.[4]

This is hardly to say that the great artists of any art from Homer on have not been seeking the deeper reality. In the high art of the twentieth century, however, the goal has been to reach, to define this reality *differently* from approaches and methods employed in the past. (Of course the twentieth-century artists build upon the experience of the late nineteenth century—Baudelaire, Monet, Henry James are only a few of the "creators" of twentieth-century art.) The human being in his infinite variety and beauty, both external and internal, is not lost sight of but is viewed, in our era, as through a prism instead of straight on. In Picasso's etchings "The Sculptor's Studio," we see the conventionally beautiful model studying her Cubist representation, as rendered by the artist, who looks like the famous Hellenistic portraits of Homer. The model shows no surprise at all at seeing herself in a Cubist abstraction. It is simply a different rendering from the way a beautiful person would have been captured in the past. The Cubist depiction serves remarkably well, however, "to extend our normal consciousness" of what it means to be a human being.[5]

Thus this book attempts to study significant examples of truly modern art that are enhanced by, combined with, classical motifs; or, as in the cases of Broch and Yourcenar, works of modern art that are wholly concerned with classical subjects. This is a narrow focus, and the omissions will strike the reader. A more ambitious study would have embraced both Joyce's *Ulysses* and Eliot's *The Waste Land*, those two path-finding works of 1922. The latter, however, is in the repertory of every scholar of modernism; the former has been subjected to the deepest scrutiny. Thus I chose to use the lesser-known novel by Hermann Broch, *The Death of Vergil*, instead of Joyce's work; my principal salute to Eliot is in terms of his play *The Family Reunion*.

Many successful works, such as Robinson Jeffers's *Medea*, Judith Anderson's famous vehicle of 1947, I took as too derivative and not works of truly modern art as I define it. I debated at length, however, about including Eugene O'Neill's *Mourning Becomes Electra* (1931). This play is a work of great imagination, with powerful Freudian undercurrents. Yet it strikes me as old-fashioned, more in the spirit of the nineteenth century (its actual setting) than ours. I think that today's audiences would rather see a fine production of Aeschylus's *Oresteia* itself.

There was the temptation to do an omnibus review of the historical novels of Mary Renault. These works also, however, are reconstructions and are not examples of modern art according to my restricted definition. (Renault's works, from *The King Must Die* in 1958 to *Funeral Games* of 1981, do speak to us today from the standpoint of the prominence of widespread archaeological discovery in Greece and the Aegean during this century.)

Beginning with Thomas Mann's novella of 1912, *Death in Venice*, we have a work drenched in classical allusion. The metamorphosis undergone by the hero of the tale, Gustav von Aschenbach, can be seen as a personal triumph as he becomes a monumental ancient figure like Menelaus of Sparta or Pentheus of Thebes. It is the exaltation of this great art critic to identify with a living work of art, the boy Tadzio. Mann's lover and his beloved accord well with our modern understanding of Greek pederasty.

A little later in our era, Pablo Picasso took up classical themes, inspired greatly by a trip to Italy in 1917. In Picasso's abundant use of the minotaur there is a reflection of the worldwide interest in Arthur Evans's excavations on Crete. The minotaur merges with the bull in *Guernica*. It emerges as the representation of the power of art in paintings of the late 1930s.

Throughout the 1930s and into the 1940s a number of play-wrights were using Greek motifs. Surrealism in all of its aspects imbues these works with a strong and unique tenor. In Gide's *Oedipus* we have the king as a family man, with full portraits given of his children. It is Cocteau in *The Infernal Machine* who provides a wonderfully fleshed-out Jocasta. The characters of these authors merge increasingly into personalities which belong to the Zeitgeist of the 1930s in Cocteau's *Orpheus* and Giraudoux's *Tiger at the Gates*. It is Eliot's triumph to use completely modern figures and a modern scene in *The Family Reunion*, with all of its surrealist reflection of *The Oresteia*.

Throughout this book there is attention paid to a Europe going to pieces and the rise of the great modern tyrannies. Hermann Broch's *The Death of Vergil* offers the mirror of art to both a modern Europe under tyrants and the parallel world of Augustus Caesar as described so well by Ronald Syme in his *The Roman Revolution*. Broch's Vergil both well reflects the ancient *vitae* of the poet and is as many-faceted as a Picasso portrait.

We now move into the second half of the century, when people truly know little Latin and less Greek. Even T. S. Eliot for a time divorces himself from classical allusion. But then came the end of World War II and the recovery of Europe. Three American writers went to the classical lands and came away with a reaction little attuned to myth but greatly attuned to the classical landscape and the meaning of that world for today.

The book concludes with a study of the works of the person who possibly is the quintessential modern "classical" artist, Marguerite Yourcenar. Her Hadrian is the ultimate extension and the "brother" of Mann's Aschenbach, Picasso's Sculptor in the Studio, Eliot's Harry, Broch's Vergil, the observing American poets.

In the autumn of 1983 the essays of Picasso, Yourcenar, and the three American poets existed as papers first conceived as public lectures. The Yourcenar study had been accepted for publication in *Classical and Modern Literature*. The poetry and plays of T. S. Eliot had long been of interest to me. Upon seeing Picasso's *Guernica* in its new and final home in Madrid in the summer of 1983, I decided to collect the thoughts and short papers of the past twenty years into a volume on classicism and modern art. The essays on Mann, the theater of the 1930s, and Broch—studies long considered—were composed for this book.

This book, then, is not a bridge across the twentieth century. It is a group of selected stepping stones. The book builds on the rather brief final chapter of Gilbert Highet's *The Classical Tradition*. I salute as a parallel work Lillian Feder's *Ancient Myth in Modern Poetry* (1971).

The bibliography needs an explanation. It contains many works that are not cited in the notes, but these works have been much consulted during the past several years. The reader who examines part 2 of the bibliography will see the seeds of many of my observations and points of view. For example, in my discussion of the poems, plays, and novels, and the works of Picasso with which the book is concerned, there is a recurring consideration of greatness, monumentality, the immortality of art. The life and work of Kenneth Clark have been a major inspiration to me, and so I include his brilliant essay *What Is a Masterpiece?*, the Walter Neurath Lecture for 1979. In his brief but sweeping analysis Clark includes the *Guernica*. I found Kenneth Clark's interest in

Picasso's famous picture inspiring and encouraging. Other works in the bibliography have had a similar value. They will be useful to other students of classicism and the artistic achievement of the twentieth century.

I very much hope that others will build upon this collection of studies. I offer the essays as a prolegomenon to a wider and deeper study of the classical presence in the arts of our era.

CHAPTER ONE

The Olympian World of Thomas Mann

Und dann sprach er das Feinste aus, der verschlagene Hofmacher: Dies, dass der Liebende göttlicher sei, als der Geliebte, weil in jenem der Gott sei, nicht aber in andern.

And then, sly arch-lover that he was, he said the subtlest thing of all: that the lover was nearer the divine than the beloved; for the god was in the one but not in the other.

—Thomas Mann, *Death in Venice*

And remember, she said, that it is when he looks upon beauty's visible presentment, and only then, that a man will be quickened with the true, and not the seeming, virtue—for it is virtue's self that quickens him, not virtue's semblance. And when he has brought forth and reared this perfect virtue, he shall be called the friend of god, and if ever it is given to man to put on immortality, it shall be given to him.

—Plato, *Symposium*

The heart of Thomas Mann's famous novella of 1912, *Death in Venice,* comes in the passages derived from or closely related to the dialogues of Plato, in particular the *Phaedrus* and the *Symposium.*[1] The great German writer Gustav von Aschenbach, during his holiday in Venice, has become enchanted with a beautiful boy, the fourteen-year-old Tadzio from Poland. Tadzio is with his mother and sisters in the same luxurious hotel on the Lido where Aschenbach is staying. While waiting for dinner to be announced at the end of his first day, Aschenbach observes the Polish family and is astonished at the boy's "perfect beauty" (STD 396, AE 485).

From this moment, Mann causes his tale of enchantment, destruction, and transformation to be infused with vivid Greek motifs from classical art and literature. The boy Tadzio is seen as the statue of the Capitoline Thorn-Puller (STD 397, AE 486), as a "little Phaeacian" (STD 399, AE 489), with the "head of Eros" in Parian marble (STD 399, AE 490). At first, the learned Aschenbach studies and enjoys the boy from the point of view of the connoisseur (STD 400, AE 490). He is utterly charmed when one day on the beach Tadzio's friend Jaschiu embraces the boy and kisses him (STD 402, AE 494). Thinking with a smile, Aschenbach warns, "But you, Critobulus, . . . you I advise to take a year's leave. That long, at least, you will need for complete recovery" (STD 402, AE 494–95). When we reflect that Critobulus was the son of Socrates' friend Crito and was present at Socrates' trial and at his death, it seems clear that Mann intends to represent Aschenbach as Socrates to the youth Tadzio.[2]

Mann proceeds to elevate Aschenbach further not by a Greek but by a Germanic allusion. Although Aschenbach had decided to leave Venice, the mishandling of his luggage forced him to return to the hotel on the Lido. He is glad to return to the calm luxury of the hotel, especially when he considers his usual summer vacation at his mountain chalet in Germany. "There clouds hung low and trailed through the garden, violent storms extinguished the light of the house at night, and the ravens he fed swung in the tops of the fir trees" (STD 410, AE 506–7). In the mountains, in that "theatre of his summer labours" (STD 410, AE 506), the great writer is the god himself, Wotan.[3] On the coast of the Adriatic this summer, however, Aschenbach, Mann immediately suggests, is not Wotan but rather a Greek figure of almost divine stature; he is like Menelaus at the moment in the *Odyssey*

(4.563–68) when Proteus predicts the eventual apotheosis of the king of Sparta.[4] And thus Aschenbach begins his own special Odyssey, a prelude for which was struck earlier as Aschenbach saw the late-rising Tadzio as a little Phaeacian (STD 399, AE 489) and thought of the Homeric passage where King Alcinoös tells Odysseus of their happy life in Phaeacia, which includes "changes of clothing and our hot baths and beds" (*Odyssey* 8.249).[5] Aschenbach's admiration for Tadzio quickens and deepens. He is alert to every feature, every detail of the boy's enchanting form (STD 411, AE 509). Aschenbach told himself that "what he saw was beauty's very essence; form as divine thought, the single and pure perfection which resides in the mind, of which an image and likeness, rare and holy, was here raised up for adoration" (STD 412, AE 510). As our devotee so speculates, he is set afire "with pain and longing" (STD 412, AE 510).[6]

"There was the ancient plane-tree outside the walls of Athens . . . here Socrates held forth to youthful Phaedrus upon the nature of virtue and desire" (Plato, *Phaedrus* 230b–c; STD 412, AE 510–11). And so begins a great moment in the life of the classical tradition in the twentieth century, the moment near the actual center of Mann's story, where the dialogues of Plato are invoked, and his hero, Socrates. From this point on classical references and themes abound in Mann's tale, but the heart of the novella is here, I believe, in the "Phaedrus passage," embracing as it does concepts taken from the *Symposium* as well as the *Phaedrus*, but especially the *Symposium*.

Plato's *Symposium* is especially important to the Phaedrus passage, the *Symposium* being Plato's most extended discourse on the nature of love and beauty. To summarize briefly, the setting of the *Symposium* is a dinner party. As the evening deepens, the conversation turns to the subject of Eros. The various guests and their host, Agathon, express in lucid, straightforward terms their understanding of the nature of Love. The views range from the idealism of Phaedrus, who extolls the friendship of Achilles and Patroclus (*Symposium* 180a–b), to the concept of the physician, Eryximachus, that love is the same as the harmony of the body in health (187a–e), to the candid view of Aristophanes that love is sexual fulfillment (191c–192c). The opinions of Pausanias and Agathon are interspersed among these speeches, and finally all attention turns to Socrates. At the beginning of the discussion, Socrates had announced that love is the one thing in the world he understands (177d–e). Now that it is his turn, however, Socrates confesses that he learned the philosophy of love from a woman of great knowledge, Diotima of Mantinea (210d).

The Phaedrus passage in *Death in Venice* bears a particularly close resemblance to the pronouncements of Diotima in the *Symposium*. It is at the end of Socrates' discourse, as informed by Diotima, that Plato gives us the image of the "heavenly ladder" as the way to an understanding of Beauty (211c). Diotima-Socrates observes,

> But if it were given to man to gaze on beauty's very self—
> unsullied, unalloyed, and freed from the mortal taint that
> haunts the frailer loveliness of flesh and blood—if, I say, it were
> given to man to see the heavenly beauty face to face, would you
> call *his*, she asked me, an unenviable life, whose eyes had been
> open to the vision, and who had gazed upon it in true con-
> templation until it had become his own forever? And re-
> member, she said, that it is when he looks upon beauty's visible
> presentment, and only then, that a man will be quickened with

the true, and not the seeming, virtue—for it is virtue's self that quickens him, not virtue's semblance. And when he has brought forth and reared this perfect virtue, he shall be called the friend of god, and if ever it is given to man to put on immortality, it shall be given to him. (211e–212a)

The Phaedrus passage also has its parallels in Plato's *Phaedrus* itself, especially the following statement in Socrates' speech to Phaedrus:

Beauty . . . we apprehend . . . through the clearest of our senses, clear and resplendent. For sight is the keenest mode of perception, vouchsafed us through the body; wisdom, indeed, we cannot see thereby—how passionate had been our desire for her, if she had granted us so clear an image of herself to gaze upon—nor yet any other of those beloved objects, save only beauty; for beauty alone this has been ordained, to be most manifest to sense and most lovely of them all. (*Phaedrus* 250d)

In his own synthetic way Thomas Mann re-creates, and re-fashions, these visionary utterances of Plato into a single powerful conception in the rapidly moving mind of Gustav van Aschenbach, as Aschenbach considers his enchantment with Tadzio:

"For beauty, my Phaedrus, beauty alone is lovely and visible at once. For, mark you, it is the sole aspect of the spiritual which we can perceive through our senses, or bear so to perceive. Else what should become of us, if the divine, if reason and virtue and truth, were to speak to us through the senses? Should we not perish and be consumed by love, as Semele aforetime was by Zeus? So beauty, then, is the beauty-lover's way to the spirit—but only the way, only the means, my little Phaedrus." . . . And then, sly arch-lover that he was, he said the subtlest thing of all: that the lover was nearer the divine than

the beloved; for the god was in the one but not in the other—
perhaps the tenderest, most mocking thought that ever was
thought, and source of all the guile and secret bliss the lover
knows. (STD 413, AE 511–12)

The concept of the lover being nearer the divine than the
beloved comes from Phaedrus's own speech in the *Symposium*, as he praises Achilles' love for Patroclus (180a). In
blending the concepts of the "heavenly ladder" speech of
Diotima-Socrates with the views of Phaedrus in the *Symposium*, Aschenbach allows the perception of beauty in the
here and now to be a supreme accomplishment. He adorns,
and magnifies, his feelings by associating them with Plato's
"heavenly ladder," forgetting that in Plato the perception of
beauty in the here and now is only the first rung of the
ladder.

Nevertheless, in Aschenbach's mind he is a divine lover,
and thus Wotan merges with Menelaus to become the supreme lover, Zeus (father of Helen, wife of Menelaus). Having come to this Platonically inspired self-description (self-deception), Aschenbach is moved to demonstrate his power
by writing a brilliant essay on a question of art and taste that
recently has come before the intellectual world during his
stay in Venice. The essay will be written in Tadzio's presence; Tadzio will be Ganymede to his Zeus: "This lad should
be in a sense his model, his style should follow the lines of
this figure that seemed to him divine; he would snatch up
this beauty into the realms of the mind, as once the eagle
bore the Trojan shepherd aloft" (STD 413, AE 512).[7] In thus
seeing himself as a god, a very Zeus, Aschenbach has moved
from the lonely votary before the altar of art, an officiating
priest, so to speak, working daily at his desk adorned with
tall wax candles in silver candlesticks, as he is described ear-

lier in the novel (STD 384, AE 464), to the position of the wor-
shipped god himself. His essay, indeed, will soon be the
wonder and admiration of the multitude (STD 414, AE 512).
Aschenbach's enchantment with Tadzio swiftly becomes a
passion. The writer comes to love the dawn of each day because soon thereafter he will see Tadzio. The sunrise is peopled for Aschenbach with figures worthy of an exuberant
painting by Poussin, as Eos, the Dawn, approaches, she the
lover of Cleitos, Cephalus, and Orion (STD 415, AE 515).[8]
As Aschenbach here relates himself to the divine dawn-
lover, Eos, soon he sees himself as the sun god, Apollo. Tadzio is compared to Hyacinthus, a victim of the love of Apollo.
(The corresponding passage in Ovid is very sensual as the
god and the beautiful youth strip for the hurling of the discus [Metamorphoses 10.176–85]. Apollo's discus strikes the
ground and bounces with a fatal blow to the beloved Hyacinthus. It was a breeze from Zephyrus, rival to Apollo for
Hyacinthus, that turned the discus. Thus a lovers' quarrel, an
innocent victim.) The underlying point here is that Aschenbach sees himself as a divine lover in every sense, whether
as god or goddess.

From this moment on Aschenbach is infatuated. It is when
his eyes meet the eyes of Tadzio in a service in San Marco
(STD 420, AE 522) that there approaches a holy consumma-
tion of their love. Soon thereafter Aschenbach, the lovelorn,
leans one night in misery against the door of Tadzio's room
(STD 421, AE 525) in the attitude known so well in the para-
clausithyron ("doorway lament") of Roman poetry, as in the
elegies of Propertius (cf. 1.16.16–48).

Aschenbach regards himself in the service of Eros, a role
not to be despised. "For Eros had received most counte-
nance among the most valiant nations—yes, were we not
told that in their cities prowess made him flourish exceed-

ingly? And many heroes of olden time had willingly borne his yoke . . . vows, prostrations, self-abasements, these were no source of shame to the lover; rather they heaped him with praise and honour" (STD 422, AE 526). Comparable is the speech of Phaedrus in the *Symposium* (178e–179a):

> If only, then, a city or an army could be composed of none but lover and beloved, how could they deserve better of the country than by shunning all that is base, in mutual emulation? And men like these fighting shoulder to shoulder, few as they were, might conquer—I had almost said—the whole world in arms. . . . Nor is there any lover so faint of heart that he would desert his beloved or fail to help him in the hour of peril, for the very presence of Love kindles the same flame of valor in the faintest heart that burns in those whose courage is innate.

And thus we are brought back to Aschenbach's earliest ideal, the figure of the sometime Roman centurion, Saint Sebastian: "Forbearance in the face of fate, beauty constant under torture, are not merely passive. They are a positive achievement, an explicit triumph; and the figure of Sebastian is the most beautiful symbol, if not of art as a whole, yet certainly of the art we speak of here" (STD 384–85, AE 466). And so Aschenbach increases his own godhead, his private divinity, as he engages with Eros and contemplates his love.

The great writer sees himself as a god. (The artist in our time has more than once been viewed as a god—Mann anticipates our contemporary fascination with such figures as Van Gogh, T. S. Eliot, Sartre, Dylan Thomas, and Jackson Pollock, all of whom suffered great vicissitudes.) For Mann's Aschenbach, however, it is an exaggeration to view himself as either Socrates or Saint Sebastian, and he has a nightmare.

The growing presence in Venice, and on the Lido, of Asiatic cholera is coincident with, and also symbolic of, Aschenbach's condition. Mann creates the atmosphere of the cholera (STD 428, AE 536–37) with a skill equal to Thucydides (2.47–54) and Lucretius (6.1138–1286) in dealing with the famous plague at Athens at the beginning of the Peloponnesian War. Our hero learns of the plague, but he stays on in Venice, mesmerized as he is by Tadzio and all that Tadzio represents.

"That night he had a fearful dream" (STD 430, AE 539). What follows is a brilliant paraphrase of, elaboration on, the two memorable passages in Euripides' drama *The Bacchae* that are concerned with the rites of the worshippers of Dionysus (*Bacchae* 677–774) and the destruction of their enemy, the Theban king Pentheus (1043–1152).[9] In Aschenbach's dream he is part of a ritual presided over by "the stranger god" (STD 430, AE 540). The orgiastic cult scene that follows is, for Mann, Euripides by way of Rohde.[10] The power of the scene, however derivative, is enthralling and worthy of the great Euripidean original.

The two unforgettable passages in *The Bacchae* are the shepherd-messenger's description of the Dionysian rite and the later messenger's report of the death of Pentheus. The high point of the former, in William Arrowsmith's translation, is as follows:

> Then at a signal
> all the Bacchae whirled their wands for the revels
> to begin. With one voice they cried aloud:
> "O Iacchus! Son of Zeus!" "O Bromius!" they cried
> until the beasts and all the mountain seemed
> wild with divinity. And when they ran,
> everything ran with them.
>
> (Euripides, *Bacchae*, 723–27)

Later, the ritual-death of King Pentheus begins as follows:

> With that, thousands of hands
> tore the fir tree from the earth, and down, down
> from his high perch fell Pentheus, tumbling
> to the ground, sobbing and screaming as he fell,
> for he knew his end was near.
>
> (1109–13)

From a similar nightmare Aschenbach awakes "unhinged" (STD 431, AE 541) and proceeds to follow the bent of his ruin, at the same time his transformation.

Aschenbach allows his appearance to be changed by a bar-ber-cosmetician as readily as the hypnotized Pentheus takes on the attributes demanded by Dionysus (whereas Pentheus becomes a woman, Aschenbach, it should be noted, en-deavors to be a younger man). The change is great, and as Aschenbach proceeds in a daze from the barber's shop, he hears the flapping of wings of harpies (STD 433, AE 544; cf. Vergil, *Aeneid* 3.210–18).

In a besotted state of mind, the great writer, supreme prose artist, sits and considers himself. He thinks of Phae-drus again, and addresses him. Aschenbach the artist-lover has fallen prey to Eros and is on the edge of an abyss (STD 434–35, AE 546–47; *Phaedrus* 251e–252a). Aschenbach has not succeeded in leaving behind the appreciation of physical beauty in order to ascend Diotima's ladder of the under-standing and comprehension of Beauty itself.

Aschenbach returns to the beach one more time, having learned that the Polish family is about to leave. Within view of his deck chair is a camera on a tripod, unattended. The bully, Jaschiu, and Tadzio are quarreling on the beach. Tad-zio is about to have his head buried in the sand.

Soon thereafter, Tadzio walks the beach alone. The lagoon, the Adriatic, stretch before the boy and Aschenbach. To the artist, steeped in classical culture, Tadzio is a veritable Psychagog (STD 437, AE 550), Hermes himself, the escort-god to the underworld (Homer, *Iliad* 24.437f.). "Some minutes passed before anyone hastened to the aid of the elderly man sitting there collapsed in his chair. They bore him to his room. And before nightfall a shocked and respectful world received the news of his decease" (STD 437, AE 550).

Thus dies Aschenbach, thus ends one of the richest works of twentieth-century art to be imbued with classical motifs of the greatest significance. Homer, Euripides, Plato, with the spirit of Socrates over all—in *Death in Venice* we have one of the great *atria* of the mind in the life of the classical tradition.

Is Aschenbach's end a fall or a transcendence? Peter Heller sees "Erfrischung [refreshment] durch Regression" as the ironic fundamental theme of the entire novella. Heller sees Mann's tale as expressive of "Kulturpessimismus," of the type, I would suggest, that we also see in Eliot's *The Waste Land*. The grandeur of Western art and letters does not sustain Gustav von Aschenbach at a critical point in his life, and thus we have in the story the "disintegration of artistic sublimation."[11]

Ernst Schmidt regards Aschenbach's history as one of the decline into the sensual; Aschenbach's Plato-Socrates is not the true voice of the *Dialogues*, it is the voice Aschenbach wants to hear. Platonism becomes an excuse for a pagan sensual orgy. Putting it slightly differently, ecstasy becomes the synthesis, for Aschenbach, of Platonism and paganism, in the name of Eros.[12]

On the other hand, the death of Gustav von Aschenbach, with Hermes Psychopompos before him and the many ideas of Homer, Plato, and Euripides behind him, can be viewed as a metamorphic triumph. Herbert Lehnert's eloquent summary must be noted:

> At this fatal moment, Aschenbach has been completely absorbed into the mythical world. His fate is experienced by the reader in such a way that his moral fall, his physical illness, the psychological development of his deadly attachment to the boy Tadzio, and his death are superseded and redeemed by the transformation of his former closed, strained, tense existence into one that is open to the mythical world, a transformation for which the price of death does not seem too high.[13]

Although Mann's hero does not ascend Diotima's "heavenly ladder," he has had, indeed, a larger than usual life. Aschenbach has written of Frederick the Great and a novel of great power, *Maia*. His judgment on matters of art is supreme and respected by the scholarly world. He knows the powers of Wotan and Socrates. At the end of his life he sees a beautiful being who fulfills his artist's dreams. Aschenbach's flaw at this point is in trying to relate personally to the rare young Tadzio. As he sits by the sea at the end, Aschenbach is released from any further effort. Aschenbach, I would suggest, does not "fall," nor is his enchantment with Tadzio "deadly." In Venice, Aschenbach's understanding of perfection in this world comes into focus for one brilliantly graphic moment, as through a camera. It is, in fact, a photographer's camera, momentarily abandoned on the beach, which is the penultimate symbol, the suggestion of Hermes being the last, in Thomas Mann's novella. The camera, the god—past and present—are joined in perfect fusion in *Death in Venice*.

CHAPTER TWO

The Resonant World
of Pablo Picasso

I t is in Pablo Picasso's *Minotauromachy* (1935) that we have the picture that is as arresting and as provocative as the masterpieces of literature and music in this century that deal with or treat classical themes. Picasso's interest in the minotaur begins to approach the crescendo of *Minotauromachy* in two voluptuous India-ink drawings of 1933 depicting nude women in the embrace of large, insistent minotaurs.[1] If the minotaur is to be related to the national spectacle of Spain, the bullfight, then the bull theme goes back to the artist's childhood and his earliest painting, *Picador* (Rubin 16), from 1889–90 (Picasso was born in 1881), and the pencil drawing *Bullfight* from 1890 (Rubin 17). Picasso's first minotaur is presented in January 1928, by way of collage in which a charcoal drawing of a man's running legs is topped by the head of a bull, the suggestion of a torso being made by pieces of pasted paper (Rubin 253, 270). The shaggy-headed minotaur that is characteristic of Picasso's handling of the beast comes in May 1933 with Picasso's cover design for the new magazine *Minotaure* (Rubin 306, 317), which had its first issue on 1 June 1933, published by Albert Skira.

It is a noteworthy coincidence that it was in this period (1921–36) that Sir Arthur Evans was publishing what by 1936 would be a four-volume study (in seven bound books) of his famous excavation on Crete at Knossos, begun in 1900. Evans, convinced as he was that the palatial labyrinth he had discovered fitted perfectly the legend of Theseus and the Minotaur, called his book *The Palace of Minos*. Picasso made a point of seldom commenting on his sources of inspiration, but the work of Sir Arthur Evans was the subject of world-wide interest, accounts frequently appearing in European newspapers.

In 1900–1902, the years of major excavation, Evans discovered the picture—the fragments of a mural—today variously known as the Bull Dance Fresco or the Bull-Leap Fresco, grouped by Evans with the several "Taureador Frescoes."[2] It was this painting that seemed to explain the feature of the legend of the Minotaur, wherein the Athenian hostages, annual tribute to King Minos, were fed to the Minotaur in the heart of Minos's palace. Now that we have Evans's fresco, it would appear that the Greek hostages very likely were compelled to learn to do acrobatic leaps over large, prancing bulls, with many of the young people losing their lives in the process. Picasso's *Minotauromachy* has all of the menace suggested by the Minoan fresco. At the same time, the etching alludes to later factors in Western culture, especially circa 1935.

The government of Nazi Germany repudiated, in 1935, the Versailles Treaty. In the same year, Mussolini's Italy invaded Abyssinia. Europe was deeply troubled, more so than many realized. In the spring of 1935 Picasso produced *Minotauromachy*. As in the near future Picasso's art would react to the dictatorship of Franco, so here the artist turns the iconography of the bullfight (the female matador lies unconscious, breasts exposed, across the back of a prancing horse), which imagery he had used so frequently, and the image of the minotaur into the larger purpose of a commentary on civilization.

In this work the minotaur is brute force, reaching to extinguish the light held by the young girl. She stands fast, her firm stance and her "classic" profile presenting all the strength of a caryatid from the Erechtheum. Behind her is the nearly naked, bearded man climbing a ladder. In his heroic seminudity (he is even barefooted), the man is classical Greece, or Old Europe, in retreat. The girl, in her English-looking coat and tam-o-shanter, is Young Europe, in whom Picasso seems to have hope (remember, this is a pre-Franco work). The passivity of Culture in the face of Barbarism is represented by the two majas in the window, and by the lifeless matador. Picasso suggests Culture by the reference to an old-master painting (very likely Goya's *Majas on a Balcony*) and by a figure of the matador from the famous sport of the bullfight. The sea and the sailing vessel on the horizon sum up the world of the Mediterranean from Minoan times to the present.

The effect on the viewer of *Minotauromachy* is that of a dream, or a nightmare. The etching is, in fact, a culmination in Picasso's work in the style of surrealism (*Guernica* will be the masterpiece of this period in Picasso's creative life). It was after 1927 that Picasso's work began to have surrealist features,[3] although in general Picasso was never a "member" of the surrealist movement, as were the poets Paul Eluard and André Breton, and the painters Joan Miró and Max Ernst. Nevertheless, *Minotauromachy* is one of the great surrealist achievements. The etching clearly has overtones of or origins in some of the artist's surrealist work of 1934, the four plates in the *Suite Vollard* called "The Blind Minotaur."[4] Here a pathetic monster stalks along beaches viewed by classical-looking men, women, and children.

The *Suite Vollard* is one of the grand collections of graphic art in the history of art. The one hundred plates, mostly etchings, were made by Picasso between 1930 and 1937 on the express command of the publisher, Ambroise Vollard. In the *Suite,* plates 1–27 are of mixed subjects, including the dramatic aquatint "Satyr and Sleeping Woman" (1936), a variation on the minotaur theme.[5] Plates 28–32 are entitled "Battle of Love" and depict gigantic copulations. Plates 83–93, devoted to "The Minotaur" (all from 1933), are followed by the "The Blind Minotaur," plates 94–97. The collection ends, not undeservedly, with the three portraits of Vollard (plates 98–100).

It is the central section, plates 37–82, from 1933–34, "The Sculptor's Studio," which gives us one of the most impressive works of this century to be inspired by classical antiquity.[6] As is well known, Picasso had a major aesthetic experience in becoming acquainted with ancient art during his trip to Rome in 1917. In the course of his trip, he also visited Naples and Pompeii. Scores of works followed filled with classical—neoclassical?—figures. With regard to the etchings and lithographs from this classical period, Hans Bolliger observes, "The neoclassical manner developed in these works, for the most part line drawings, was to run like a red thread through all of Picasso's successive styles."[7]

The suite of "The Sculptor's Studio" comprises forty-six plates, all concerned with the glorification of art and the artist. Picasso was preoccupied with sculpture at this time and was in the position to review his activity of the last thirty years.[8] In the series the artist is depicted as a nude sage, his bearded face combining the appearance in ancient art of both Socrates and Aristotle. Heroically nude, the artist is a god.

The model is voluptuously beautiful, with the benign fea-

Pablo Picasso, *Guernica*. May–early June 1937. Oil on canvas, 11'5½" × 25'¾". Collection, The Prado, Madrid. Bequest of the artist. Copyright ARS N.Y. / SPADEM, 1988.

Pablo Picasso, *Guernica* (detail). May–early June 1937. Oil on canvas. Collection, The Prado, Madrid. Bequest of the artist. Copyright ARS N.Y. / SPADEM, 1988.

Pablo Picasso, *Guernica* (detail). May–early June 1937. Oil on canvas.
Collection, The Prado, Madrid. Bequest of the artist. Copyright ARS
N.Y. / SPADEM, 1988.

tures of an ancient Venus or Juno. She stares calmly at her representations, so often rendered in high Cubist fashion (Bolliger, plate 38). Sometimes there is company in the studio (plate 41); on one occasion the model has a female friend with her, studying blandly the work of art (plate 42). The sculptor can wonder at his own work (plate 49); he and the model can marvel at his more complex groups (plates 54, 55, and a group similar in power to the Dirce in the National Museum in Naples, plate 57). The tone, or mood, in these plates is worthy of the east end of the Parthenon Frieze, where gods and men commingle at the moment of the folding (unfolding?) of the sacred peplos. Serenity, confidence, and happiness are in the air. The difference is that Picasso presents the privacy of an atelier, whereas the Frieze deals with a moment as cosmic as it is public.

The climax of Picasso's suite comes in plates 73 and 74, where, in 73, the model surveys a sculptured torso reminiscent of the Venus di Milo, while in 74 she looks at herself in a life-size Cubist creation, the body abstracted. These two plates side by side sum up Western art from the Hellenistic era to the twentieth century. The progress of art in this great passage of time has been from Naturalism to Cubism. Realism finally gave way to Impressionism. There was the question, What is really real? Cubism offered a succinct answer.

"The Sculptor's Studio" concludes with an etching (plate 82) richly executed in combined technique showing four women before a Zeus-like bust of the artist. The women range from a statuesque seated figure resembling the figures in the east pediment of the Parthenon to a diademed odalisque worthy of Ingres. Two figures recline, each with the features of Cubist sculpture. The picture is a summing up of art through the ages, the artist himself in a niche, atop a fluted column. The print clearly is a declaration of Picasso's understanding of the development of Western art, and of his own self-conscious awareness of the special role of the artist in all civilization. Here in the *Suite Vollard* Pablo Picasso and Thomas Mann have the same view concerning "the present-day vitality of the classical tradition."

The trip to Italy in 1917, including a stay on the Via Margutta in Rome for eight weeks (Rubin 196–97), was a momentous experience in the life of Picasso. It is in 1920 that the first neoclassical works begin to appear, notably a pencil drawing of Nessus and Dejanira (Rubin 226). There follow such other "Hellenistic" works as the monumental oil painting of 1921, *Three Women at the Spring* (Rubin 233), the women with faces of the Venus di Milo and dresses as voluminous as on the Parthenon figures. Picasso continued to work in the neoclassical vein, in 1922 painting the picture of two enthusiastic dancers, *Women Running on the Beach* (Rubin 238) and in 1923 his *kouroi,* two sturdy young men, one of whom is playing *The Pipes of Pan* (Rubin 239). (Both of these pictures suggest the manner of the dancer Isadora Duncan. The famous photograph of her posed in ecstasy on the porch of the Parthenon was made by Edward Steichen in 1921.) It was also in 1923 that Picasso painted his much-reproduced *Woman in White* (Rubin 242), the calm and gracious figure very like an Athenian grave monument of the fourth century B.C. In the summer of 1925 comes a hint of "The Sculptor's Studio" in the oil *Studio with Plaster Head,* a still life focusing on the bust and limbs of a Hellenistic or Roman heroic statue (Rubin 250). It needs to be observed, however, that Picasso's Cubist work continued unabated in this period. Indeed, what may be his most popular Cubist work, *Three Musicians,* dates from 1921. It was more in the

Pablo Picasso, *Nessus and Dejanira*. September 1920. Pencil, 8¼″ ×
10¼″. Collection, The Museum of Modern Art, New York. Acquired
through the Lillie P. Bliss Bequest.

Pablo Picasso, *Myrrhina and Kinesias* from *Lysistrata* by Aristophanes. The Limited Edition Club, 1934. Etching, 8⅝″ × 6″. Collection, The Museum of Modern Art, New York. The Louis E. Stern Collection.

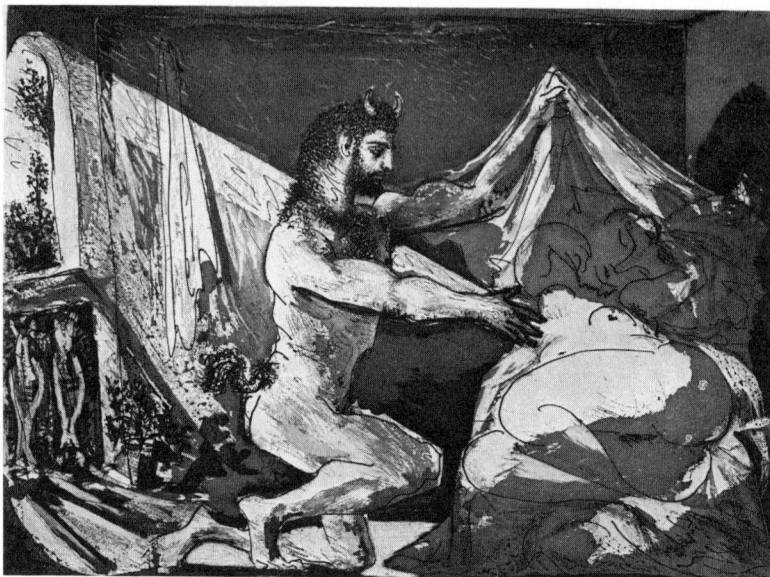

Pablo Picasso, *Faun Unveiling a Sleeping Woman* (Jupiter and Antiope, after Rembrandt). June 12, 1936. Etching and aquatint, printed in black; 12⁷⁄₁₆″ × 16⁷⁄₁₆″. Collection, The Museum of Modern Art, New York. Purchase.

Pablo Picasso, *Still Life with Red Bull's Head.* 1938. Oil on enamel on canvas, 38⅛″ × 51¼″. Collection, The Museum of Modern Art, New York. Gift of Mr. and Mrs. William A. M. Burden.

Cubist vein than the neoclassical that Picasso created his first minotaur, the collage described above, made in 1928.

Picasso's interest in the antique continued well into the ensuing decade, in the first years of which he created illustrations for two of the most beautiful books published in this century. These books are Albert Skira's production of a prose translation by Georges Lafaye of Ovid's *Metamorphoses* (1931) and the Limited Editions Club's production of Gilbert Seldes' translation of Aristophanes' *Lysistrata* (1934). For the Ovid, Picasso made thirty etchings illustrating major episodes in the *Metamorphoses,* ranging from Deucalion and Pyrrha creating a new human race to Meleager killing the Caledonian boar and concluding with Numa as a pupil of Pythagoras.[9] The etchings are strictly linear, showing the most exquisite draughtman's technique. What is more, as Horodisch emphasizes, the illustrations suit the text perfectly, making a most satisfying harmony between text and illustrations.[10] I think we can say because Picasso's own *oeuvre* displays continual variety, with one phase emerging from another, with the phenomenon we have noted, for example, of his Cubist and Neoclassical works being created simultaneously, that Picasso found the author of the *Metamorphoses* a most congenial fellow artist.

The sensuous, bawdy, psychologically probing *Lysistrata* would have had an equal appeal for Pablo Picasso. The directors of the Limited Editions Club, conservative in their artistic views, probably selected Picasso as the illustrator for their *Lysistrata* "because his Ovid etchings reflected so faithfully the commonly accepted idea of the antique."[11] In fact, however, the etchings for *Lysistrata* have a less formally elegant tone than do the etchings for the *Metamorphoses.* The nervous, sketchy pen drawings (thirty-four in number) and the six full-page etchings capture the braggadocio of both the men and the women in the play, along with the pomposity and potent sexuality of the men and the recalcitrance and potent sexuality of the women.

In the six full-page etchings Picasso is right on target in spotting key scenes in the play: Lysistrata leading the council of women; Kinesias and Myrrhine; two desperate men on the seashore; the negotiations between the Athenians and the envoys from Sparta; the celebration of peace and the reconciliation of the two sexes. Student of love that Picasso was, it is not surprising that he devoted two of the six etchings to the depiction of Myrrhine and her ardent husband. Boeck and Sabartés offer a summation of Picasso's achievement in the illustrations of these two works as they reflect generally on Picasso's draughtsmanship: "The harmonious interweaving of the white spaces among the black threads of the drawing is predominant, and anatomy is sacrificed to the expressive mobility of the limbs. This technique culminates in the etchings for Ovid's *Metamorphoses* published in 1931, in which the purity of the lines, the sparing use of shading, and the balance of the composition come close to perfection. In the etchings for Aristophanes' *Lysistrata* (1934), restrained treatment of subject matter and purely linear balance of the sheet are dropped in favor of greater decorative richness."[12]

That these two literary masterpieces should enjoy fresh translations in sumptuous editions in our century is not surprising. The ever-appealing, timeless significance of a work is what makes the work "classic" in every sense of the term. The remarkable feature of these publications is that the leading artist of the century, not singly responsible but certainly greatly responsible for the rejection of "the cult of beauty" that had dominated Western art since early Greece,[13] should turn around and provide elegant, perfect illustrations for two ancient masterpieces. In point of fact, although Picasso felt that art badly needed a new direction and offered such direction first with the painting *Les Demoiselles d'Avignon* in 1907 and then as a leader of the Cubist movement, Picasso never abandoned or lost sight of his classical heritage. It would appear that he never forgot the plaster reproductions of Greek and Roman art housed in the School of Fine Arts and Crafts in Málaga, his birthplace. That experience became part of the experience of the visit to Italy when Picasso was thirty-six years old. As Maurice Raynal has observed in discussing Picasso's classicism, "Picasso easily relieved the monotonous, impersonal forms of Classicism with that warm, spontaneous flow of self-expression which is the great constant in his career, running fresh and undiminished even in times of purely plastic research work. Throughout this period we see him handling his themes with great poetic licence, delighting in figures and texture, and achieving at the same time a classical unity of form and content—just the unity we should expect from Picasso, who seems to be a ruthless observer at one moment and a tender poet the next, and who, of course, is both at once."[14]

And so we see several of the strongest classical elements in the work of Picasso, and his continuous interest in classical antiquity. His fascination with the bullfight and the figure of the minotaur seems to be a coalescence in Picasso's mind of an appreciation of the nature of brute strength and the fragility of civilization. The artist, for Picasso, is best illustrated by a bearded Homer type, a figure out of Hellenistic antiquity. The book illustrations demonstrate cogently Picasso's sympathy with the Greco-Roman world.

Picasso continued to work with the minotaur theme in 1936. In these mainly India-ink drawings (Rubin 334–35), Picasso includes, as in *Minotauromachy,* the horse. In "Minotaur and Dead Mare Before a Grotto," the massive bull-man holds the collapsed body of a dead horse in his right arm, warning away with his left hand a classical nymph rising from behind a gigantic carved fist. The picture is somber and full of menace. In contrast, later in the year Picasso produced his "Minotaur, Horse, and Bird," in which the three figures appear to be on a high ledge. The minotaur has the body of a wrestler, the face of an angel. He stares below. The bird and the horse are anxious—to leave such an altitude?

The facts that follow are well known and are rehearsed in every book on Picasso. In July of 1936 the Spanish Civil War began. In January 1937 the Spanish government in exile commissioned Picasso to paint a mural for its pavilion at the World's Fair in Paris. On 26 April 1937 the old Basque town of Guernica was heavily bombed by Franco's forces. This brutal action was the catalyst for Picasso. The first sketch for the mural, to be called *Guernica,* is dated 1 May 1937.[15] After the Paris exhibition the picture traveled, and finally Picasso made an extended loan of the painting to the Museum of Modern Art in New York. At his death in 1973, Picasso bequeathed the picture to the Prado in Madrid, where it arrived in September 1981. The painting is now impressively hung in an annex of the Prado, the Cason del Buen Retiro.

The present writer has seen *Guernica* many times in New York and most recently, in the summer of 1983, in Madrid. Undoubtedly, the primary, or first, effect of the painting is shock,[16] whether you "read" the picture from left to right or right to left.[17] Moreover, we are at once impressed with the number of women in the picture—four of the six human forms are women in a state of shock or lamentation. Although Brendel finds this situation "rather curious," in fact he finds the Woman with the Lamp appearing as the chorus in a Greek tragedy, at the same time an onlooker.[18] Professor Brendel was on the right track. The overall tone of *Guernica* is that of shock and lamentation such as we have in Euripides' *The Trojan Women*. The Woman with the Lamp is Hecuba at Troy. She also suggests Demeter just after the discovery of the loss of Persephone in the Homeric hymn. I, too, "read" the picture from right to left. (We might observe that Picasso's stark, simplistic figures go with that early era in Greek culture when *boustrophedon*, writing from right to left and back again, was being practiced.)

After initial shock, the classicist viewing *Guernica* observes four representations that seem to be classical in origin or, and more likely, that seem to derive from classicizing works in Picasso's previous work. The Woman with the Lamp, her huge face in classical profile; the anguished horse; the fallen warrior, or toppled statue, filling the lower left half of the picture; the bull on the far left. We have seen these elements repeatedly in Picasso's work of the preceding twenty years, including the fallen warrior (toppled statue) from the 1925 oil *Studio with Plaster Head*.

It is these four figures, coming together in the *Guernica*, that make the picture such a universal statement. It is not a picture of the Basque town; there are no airplanes or soldiers' uniforms. There is the fire in the upper right-hand corner, and Raphael suggests that the fiery glow around the light bulb in the upper left center is a bomb bursting.[19] Raphael, looking for correlations between the facts and the mural, need not be right. As Brendel suggests, referring to the renowned authority on Picasso, Alfred Barr, the light can be taken as the light of day, the sun being an eye with the bulb as its pupil.[20] In point of fact, however, we do not need to say any more about the light bulb and its glow except that it puts the overall allegory into our time. (The Woman with the Lamp holds a kerosene lamp with no glow at all. I take the kerosene lamp to be a modern archaism on Picasso's part, signifying the antiquity of the Basque town and the helplessness of humanity.)

Thus, the Woman with the Lamp is the generalized woman whom we saw in the "The Sculptor's Studio." Her three fellow-women are less generalized. In their anguish they are characters out of *The Trojan Women*. The woman below the Woman with the Lamp is dumb with amazement; the woman to our right throws up her hands and screams; the woman on the far left with the dead child howls. These cries form a single scream which lasts forever. As Max Raphael says of the picture, "Mankind is reduced to a scream."[21]

Just left of center but virtually the centerpiece of the painting is the horse, his body pierced by a spear (notice, not by shrapnel or a bayonet but by an antique spear). As the classicist views *Guernica* with increasing concentration, the horse is not only the horse of the bullfight but also the animal most useful to mankind since early antiquity. Here the picture commingles the horse and the fallen warrior. We are watching the violent death of a horse and horseman from the Parthenon Frieze. We are seeing Rembrandt's *Polish Rider* and his horse suddenly made real beings and destroyed. The center of *Guernica* depicts the end of civilization.

And so to the Bull. Its body in blacks and grays, the Bull's great head and neck are white, with a white streak running down its torso. The Bull's Cubist face stares out from the canvas at the viewer (whereas the eyes of the other participants are absorbed in the catastrophe). The Bull is unmoved by the scene of death and destruction before him. The world beside him is what it is.

The *Guernica* Bull symbolizes power and strength as an absolute force. Its heavy testicles and large sharp hooves are aspects of the Bull's power. This is the bull of Minoan legend and of the fresco in the Palace of Minos. The *Guernica* Bull is not a minotuar, but it is dominant, as is the creature in *Minotauromachy*. Whereas, however, the minotaur of *Minotauromachy* faces resistance and seems to hesitate, not sure of what to do about the little girl's candle, the *Guernica* Bull in Picasso's allegory symbolizes almighty force and absolute power. The force and power are like the brute strength which devastated Guernica, but the strength in the picture transcends any particular historical moment. The Bull is part of the general statement made by the entire composition about the fragility of civilization and humanity. We are all at the mercy of the Bull.

After *Guernica*, in many estimates the picture of the century, Picasso used classical motifs with far less frequency than in the period just considered. He never, however, abandoned his interest in classical antiquity. As late as August 1967 (Picasso died at the age of ninety-one in 1973), Picasso made a pencil drawing (Rubin 447) called "Mythological Scene." A voluptuous Venus figure is seated on a throne, her attendants being a very paunchy Apollo, with bow and arrow, and a sagging, hatted Hermes. A shaggy-headed dwarf in Elizabethan costume completes the odd group. Picasso's gods were growing old.

From 1962 there is the frantic oil *Rape of the Sabines* (Rubin 444), preceded in 1957 by a mural for the UNESCO delegates' lounge in Paris, the *Fall of Icarus* (Rubin 417–18). In 1946 Picasso painted twenty-two panels for the decoration of the museum at Antibes. Among these are three panels: *Satyr, Faun, Centaur* (Rubin 381), all joyous linear compositions, simpler, however, than the work in "The Sculptor's Studio."

His interest in the bull is seen many times in the creations of the last third of Picasso's life, but these depictions have no classical overtones. It was just after *Guernica*, in 1938, that Picasso took up again the minotaur. From November of 1938 there are two still lifes in oil, each with a kind of portrait bust of a minotaur. In the painting dated 26 November, the still life consists of a candle, a pallette, and brushes resting against pages of writing, and a bull's head, more beast than man, mounted on a stand (Rubin 362). The next day, 27 November, Picasso repeated the picture, this time adding an empty picture frame and turning the bull's features into those of a man, with deep eyes and sensuous lips.[22] The minotaur has come to be the force of art, the symbol of creativity.

CHAPTER THREE

Archetypal Hellas:
The Theater of Cocteau,
Gide, Giraudoux, Eliot

Writers in the Europe of Hitler's Germany and in the first years of World War II found themselves concerned with the nature of tyranny, the causes of war, and the behavior of human beings under conditions of great stress. To the writers of this era the themes of Homer, Aeschylus, and Sophocles were congenial. Homer wrote of a world ravaged by conflict and strife. Aeschylus knew of the tyranny of the Peisistratids at Athens and the coming of the Persians. Sophocles saw the brilliant manipulations of Pericles and the creation of the Athenian Empire. In addition to these events of history, the fabulous worlds of Thebes, Mycenae, and Troy—autocratic, aristocratic, and imperial—came close to home in the Europe of the 1930s. The two decades between the two world wars were so much the final end of an *ancien régime* and the beginning of life as we know it today.

During these years the study of archaeology made great advances. In Italy, in the early 1930s, Benito Mussolini gave to such archaeologists as Amedeo Maiuri every encouragement for the recovery of the Roman world. The imperial fora in Rome, pristine Cumae, new districts in Pompeii either were brought to light or given a special enhancement. In Greece the great work of the American School of Classical

Studies at Athens was under way in the meticulous excavation of the Athenian Agora.

In general, the use of classical motifs in literature and the other arts in the years from about 1925 to 1940 was a continuation of the "classical awareness" held by all educated people for generations in the past. In the 1930s, however, there was an efflorescence of artistic interest in classical themes, for which period Picasso's *Guernica* of 1937 is the centerpiece. The influence of Eliot's *The Waste Land* and Joyce's *Ulysses,* both from 1922, was great, along with Picasso's vibrant neoclassicism as outlined earlier. These demonstrations of inspiration from classical sources, both literary and archaeological, make the era of the 1930s a vivid chapter in the history of the classical tradition.

European theater of the time shows three approaches to the use of classical motifs. There is the reconstruction of a famous classical episode as in Giraudoux's depiction of the eve of the Trojan War in *Tiger at the Gates,* or there is the recreation of a classical setting in completely modern terms as exemplified by Cocteau's *The Infernal Machine* and Eliot's *The Family Reunion,* or there is the modern version of a classical work.

André Gide's *Oedipe* (1931) is a modern version, with additions, of Sophocles' *Oedipus Tyrannos.*[1] The scene is Thebes, beset by a plague that includes both caterpillars in the fields and a violent internal ailment among a number of the people. The chorus laments. King Oedipus has sent his brother-in-law, Creon, to Delphi to consult the oracle, and Creon's return with Delphic instructions is as early as in the Sophoclean original. In due course we learn of the youth of Oedipus, spent at the court of Polybus of Corinth; his leaving that home; and his murder of the stranger on the road. It is from Jocasta herself that Oedipus learns of the identity of his real father. The suicide of Jocasta follows, and Oedipus blinds himself.

Gide's variations are the following, and they are characteristic of the work of other playwrights of the period: Oedipus is not a majestic *tyrannos;* he is the ruler but does not have an imperial aura about him. He uses ordinary language. He shows a continual concern for his family. He is more the *pater familias* than the king. In this familial context the chorus is little heard. (The brief use of the chorus in Gide's play points up the fact that not a little of the grandeur of the Sophoclean play is due to the solemn beauty of the choral odes.) The rest of the characters share in the dignified but not elevated diction of Oedipus. Teiresias is not an awesome figure. As the tutor to Antigone and Ismene, he is a family counselor. He dresses as a friar and has the familiarity of a priest in a wealthy, devout Catholic family.

The four children are present throughout, and through them Gide gives Oedipus a family life. Oedipus has been married to Jocasta for twenty years (Russell 3, Bell 57). Their sons, Polynices and Eteocles, are in their teens; so, too, Antigone. Ismene is younger. Antigone wants to become a nun (Russell 14, Bell 66). The children react to each other strongly and their sexual potency, although not emphasized by Gide, is in the air. The two boys are very alike; Eteocles remarks on how much they have in common (Russell 23, Bell 73). The two girls are very different; Ismene remarks on how much they quarrel (Russell 22, Bell 73). It appalls Creon that Eteocles is attracted sexually to Ismene (Russell 25, Bell 75).

Thus Gide's Oedipus, family man. Gide provides background such as we gain from the ancient authors only by combining the three plays of Sophocles and Aeschylus's

Seven Against Thebes. Gide's special touch is the portrayal of Polynices and Eteocles as precocious teenagers who are very much their father's children. With Gide, the royal house of Thebes becomes a momentary Buddenbrooks.[2]

A much freer and more imaginative reconstruction of Oedipus and his world is Jean Cocteau's play *La Machine infernale* (1934).[3] The special novelty of Cocteau is his full-blown portrayal of Jocasta. Cocteau's second innovation is his portrait of the Sphinx. The whole play is very much a study of Oedipus in relation to women. The portrayal of Oedipus himself is rather passive, as compared with the theatricality of Jocasta.

The opening of *The Infernal Machine,* on the ramparts of the royal castle, recalls at once the first act of *Hamlet.* Two soldiers, the one younger than the other, are on guard for a ghost, whom the Young Soldier has seen. The ghost has urged the Young Soldier to give a warning to the queen (Wildman 88, Bell 105). Enter Jocasta and Teiresias. In the stage directions, Cocteau has Jocasta speak with a strong accent, the international accent of royalty (Wildman 92, Bell 110). Throughout the play Jocasta reminds us of a grand queen of the Balkans, especially Queen Marie of Roumania, who delighted in lilies and leopard skins.[4] She affects a long scarf about her neck, trailing to the ground, such a scarf as was favored by the famous dancer Isadora Duncan, who died by strangulation in 1927, her scarf caught in the wheel of a car.

The queen is on familiar terms with Teiresias, whom she calls "Zizi." In her opening scene we learn that she has had insomnia since the death of Laius and the coming of the Sphinx. She has come to the ramparts to interview the soldier who has seen the ghost. As Jocasta interrogates the

Young Soldier, she remarks on how "he" would be the same age, nineteen, as the soldier (Wildman 97, Bell 118). The ghost appears and calls "Jocasta!" (Wildman 99, Bell 120), but no one hears him. The Young Soldier describes the ghost, with its blood-stained temple. There is the crowing of a cock as Teiresias and Jocasta depart from the ramparts down a long flight of stairs.

The second act begins in a setting of vaguely classical ruins. The Sphinx sits among the ruins, a young girl in a white dress. She is accompanied by the Egyptian god with the jackal's head, Anubis. The Sphinx expresses regret for her death-dealing life (Wildman 105–6, Bell 130–31).

A woman of Thebes, accompanied by two children, wanders in. She does not recognize the Sphinx, but she tells the Sphinx her story. One of her sons has recently died—of the Sphinx. The mother and children wander away, leaving the Sphinx saddened that the woman referred to her as a scourge (Wildman 111, Bell 111). She wishes she were dead.

Oedipus approaches. He and the Sphinx have the typical conversation of two strangers meeting. Oedipus tells his story, from Corinth to the crossroads of Delphi and Daulis. He wants to leave but obeys the command of the Sphinx to stay, close his eyes, and count to fifty. In this interval she mounts a pedestal and becomes her supreme self, the Sphinx. In the conversation that follows, the Sphinx forces Oedipus to listen to the riddle, to which she herself gives the answer. Oedipus finds the whole procedure "idiotic" (Wildman 120, Bell 150), yet she persists, and then Oedipus with his own lips answers the riddle. He dashes away crying, "Victory!" (Wildman 121, Bell 151). Oedipus returns for his trophy and carries the body of the Sphinx over his shoulders, like Heracles carrying a lion (Wildman 125, Bell 158). What he does not know is that Anubis a moment earlier gave the Sphinx the supreme satisfaction of knowing what her conqueror's fate is to be.

As act 3, "The Wedding Night," progresses, there is no cheer. Jocasta and Oedipus are exhausted from the simultaneous wedding and coronation. As they prepare for bed, Jocasta studies her husband's feet. She has a dreadful recall (Wildman 140–41, Bell 180–81). Oedipus sleeps. Jocasta rocks the cradle, which has been a feature of the room from the beginning of the act.

The fourth act, set seventeen years later, moves quickly. We learn of the death of Polybus of Corinth, and of the circumstances surrounding the death of Laius. Jocasta kills herself by hanging, with her scarf. An old shepherd tells all, as in the Sophoclean original. To the blind Oedipus Jocasta appears one more time, as ghost and mother.

Thus two modern retellings of the Oedipus myth. Gide keeps the classical setting and the serious tone, without the sober grandeur of tone, of the Sophoclean original, adding the portrayals of Oedipus's children. Cocteau presents his play in a surrealist ambience, thereby giving his characters the modernity of his time. His innovations are in the full-scale fleshing-out of Jocasta and the Sphinx. Both playwrights were compelled to include the suicide of Jocasta and the blinding of Oedipus. In this necessity, the modern versions seem pale beside the Sophoclean original. No one could possibly improve on the gripping speech of the messenger, in which we are told of the death of Jocasta, Oedipus's confrontation with her body, then his denuding of her body as he removes the brooches, with which he blinds himself.[5]

The modern author who wants to use classical motifs has

an easier time, and has the potential of more impressive
work, when the ancient legend is less detailed in the original
source. Cocteau had a better opportunity to use a myth in
accordance with his own original thinking in his earlier
work, the *Orphée* of 1925.[6] In this thoroughly surrealist
drama, Orpheus and Eurydice are a married couple absorbed in poetry. In the vein of an experiment by Marcel
Duchamp, Orpheus is trying to find a poem in the tapping of
a horse's hoof. As the play opens, Orpheus struggles to in-
terpret letters from the tapping and thinks he hears the word
merci (Savacool 106, Cocteau 23). Eurydice berates Orpheus
for having abandoned his famous art of poetry for the non-
sense of the horse-tapping. Orpheus, however, will not be
undone. He perseveres, because a little earlier the horse
had tapped out what to Orpheus is a magical line, "Lady Eurydice shall return from the underworld" ("Madame Eurydice reviendra des enfers") (Savacool 108, Cocteau 27).

Orpheus is determined to send this verse as his entry in
the approaching Thracian poetry competition. It concerns
Eurydice that Orpheus means to leave their country home
and go to the city for the competition because she knows
that Orpheus has an enemy there, the Bacchant Aglaonice.
The two quarrel, and in his anger Orpheus breaks a window
pane.

The glazier, Heurtebise, comes to install a new pane.
While Orpheus is out of the room, Eurydice and the glazier
are able to have a private conversation in which she tells
Heurtebise of her old friendship with Aglaonice. Heurtebise
reveals that he, too, has been in touch with the Bacchant,
who wants him to bring to her a letter she has sent Eurydice.

For the moment, however, Heurtebise prepares to fix the
pane, standing on a chair that Orpheus, returning, removes,

leaving the glazier suspended in air. Orpheus leaves; Eurydice discovers Heurtebise standing in the air and is thrilled by the miracle. To Heurtebise it is nothing. Eurydice then locates the letter, for which Aglaonice has given Heurtebise a special envelope. As Eurydice licks the mucilage on the envelope, she realizes that it is poisoned. She begs Heurtebise to find Orpheus.

In the following scene Death and her assistants, Azrael and Raphael, enter the room. They arrange an apparatus of thread on a bobbin. Death enters Eurydice's bedroom, and Raphael cuts the thread. The trio are modern Parcae, the three Fates.

Upon Orpheus's return with Heurtebise, he determines to go find Eurydice. It happens that Death has left behind a pair of surgeon's gloves, which Heurtebise advises Orpheus to take to Death. Orpheus, calling "Eurydice!," departs through a mirror. The gloves are a latter-day Golden Bough for Proserpina; the mirror, the river Styx, both as in the Sixth Book of Vergil's *Aeneid* (the Bough, 6.197–211; Styx, 383–416).

Orpheus returns via the mirror, Eurydice behind him. Orpheus declares to Heurtebise that the one-line poem has come true (Savacool 131, Cocteau 78). The three then sit down to lunch, with the details of serving and chatting governed by Orpheus's pact with Death that he not look at Eurydice. Here Cocteau combines the homely, the everyday, with Fate. We know that it is only a matter of time until Orpheus and Eurydice confront each other. For Orpheus the tension becomes intolerable, but the instant he looks at his wife she dissolves into the mirror.

Soon thereafter Orpheus is warned by a letter that Aglaonice has found his poem offensive[7] and has turned the jury against him; moreover, a band of Bacchants is on their way to Orpheus's home. Drums are heard, rocks fly through the windows, breaking the mirror. Orpheus goes out onto the balcony and in a moment not a rock but his severed head comes flying into the room.

In the following scene police come to investigate the murder of Orpheus. Eurydice, reappearing through the mirror, asks Heurtebise to join her and Orpheus as soon as he can. A short comical scene follows in which the talking head informs the chief of police that its name is Jean Cocteau. It is this scene of the talking head that suggests most forcibly the source of Cocteau's play in the vignette on Orpheus and Eurydice in Vergil's Aristaeus epyllion, *Georgics* 4.453–527, the tale of the beekeeper Aristaeus, his passion for Eurydice, her death, and the effort of her husband, Orpheus, to bring her back from death, his own death brought about by decapitation.

The play ends with Orpheus, Eurydice, and Heurtebise sitting down again for a meal. They are in heaven, and the meal is a sacrament. Orpheus prays for the blessing of God, who is poetry. The feeling of the scene is that of the famous sculptured relief in Naples of Hermes, Orpheus, and Eurydice. In Cocteau's play, of course, Heurtebise all along has been Hermes Psychopompos, the guide of the souls of the dead. Thus he was indispensable for the final journey of Orpheus and Eurydice.[8]

And so Gide and Cocteau give a biographical dimension to Oedipus. Cocteau particularly elaborates in modern surrealist terms the legend of Orpheus and Eurydice. Cocteau is the ingenious modernizer. His Sphinx has the solemn, ethereal quality of the female figures in the Minotaur pictures of Picasso, classical and dreamlike at the same time. His Jocasta is a brilliant composite of several regal women in the twenties and the thirties. *The Infernal Machine* is part of the high modernism of the time. It is surrealist; in its quest for essence, it is Cubist; it is completely part of the twentieth-century aesthetic. So, too, *Orphée*. It questions Art as did Marcel Duchamp. Its scenes are prismatic, Daliesque. Yet the play stays "in touch" with Vergil and Ovid.

A compatriot of Gide and Cocteau, Jean Giraudoux, was also working with classical themes in the same period. His *Amphitryon 38* of 1929 was a popular success at once, and later in English translation as a vehicle for the Lunts. It is his next classical drama, *La Guerre de Troie n'aura pas lieu* of 1935—well known in its 1955 production, in Christopher Fry's translation, as *Tiger at the Gates*—whose high tone combined with an elegance of manner goes well with Gide and Cocteau, and anticipates Eliot.

As Gide and Cocteau put Oedipus into a fuller background than the spare Sophoclean original needed to provide, so Giraudoux gives us a full-blown Troy on the eve of the Greek invasion. Book 3 of the *Iliad,* with its famous scenes "The View from the Wall" (3.141–242) and the confrontation between Helen and Paris (3.421–47), gives considerable insight both into the viewpoint of the besieged Trojans and into the nature of Helen. Giraudoux's play is so vivid and so plausible that it would seem he also had at his disposal the lost *Cypria* from the ancient Epic Cycle, a poem dealing with Helen. We must credit Giraudoux with special sensitivity for the Homeric world.[9] The play is also remarkably prophetic. In 1935 the situation in Europe was beginning to deteriorate. Nazi Germany repudiated the Versailles Treaty in 1935, and Mussolini invaded Abyssinia. In Great Britain, however, it was a festival year, the occasion of the

Silver Jubilee of George V. In the next year German troops occupied the Rhineland and the civil war in Spain began. The opening line of the play is the confident declaration of Andromache, "There's not going to be a Trojan War, Cassandra!" (Fry 1, Giraudoux 11).

Tiger at the Gates is not a long work, and its plot is simple. The characters variously discuss whether Helen should be surrendered to the Greek ambassadors, and whether their retention of Helen will mean war. There is the subordinate subject of whether Helen really wants to return to Sparta and Menelaus. The straightforward, natural quality of these conversations gives the work a Homeric directness and reality. While Andromache and Cassandra converse, Cassandra develops the image of destiny as a waking beast (specified as a tiger in Fry's translation). The beast is restive (Fry 3, Giraudoux 15). The beast is both destiny and human nature.

Hector arrives, fresh from a successful campaign in the hinterland. He learns that Andromache is pregnant. They discuss the future of their son (Andromache is confident of the child's sex) and go on to a discussion of the life of the soldier, a life which Hector describes as strangely thrilling.

Cassandra returns with Paris. Paris informs Hector that Helen is incomparable (Fry 12, Giraudoux 27–28) among the many women he has known. Cassandra dilates on the infatuation of the old men of Troy with Helen (Fry 12–13, Giraudoux 28–29). When Priam and Hecuba appear with their entourage, the Mathematician explains to Hector that Helen is a model of perfection. He declares that all truths must henceforth be measured in terms of Helen's perfect qualities (Fry 17, Giraudoux 36). The play continues with its characters discussing the nature of sexuality, love, youth, and age.

Hector soon encounters Helen, and there ensues an engrossing dialogue between Hector and Helen as to whether she is in love with Paris and with Menelaus, and the likelihood of her returning with the Greek ambassadors. Giraudoux's Helen is an intriguing portrayal of a human being living in accordance with both the laws and the caprices of nature. Helen does not know what is going to happen, nor will she make any kind of a decision that will direct the future in any way for anyone.[10]

As the second act opens, with the great Gates of War looming open in the background (an edifice and custom from Roman times), Helen attempts playfully to seduce the fifteen-year-old Troilus. The poet Demokos appears, eager to write a poem on the subject of Helen's face. Hecuba is now eager that the Gates of War be closed, but nobody is prepared to do so. Demokos opines that Troy needs a war song. Instead of the usual comparison of war with Medusa, he will compare it with Helen's face (Fry 39, Giraudoux 72).

The court continues to debate how, or how not, to receive the Greek embassy. The expert on international law, Busiris, has many points of view. Vexed by all this indecision, Hector finally closes the Gates of War (Fry 49, Giraudoux 86). At that instant, a messenger comes to announce the landing of Ulysses and his party.

The first of the Greeks to enter the palace is the blustering Ajax. He is viciously harsh toward Hector and also to Demokos, striking both of them on the face. A calmer and more diplomatic Ulysses arrives, with his ultimatum: Helen is to be returned to the Greeks within the hour (Fry 59, Giraudoux 106). There is, however, the question of Helen's chastity since she has been with Paris. Menelaus wants her as she was. There is much discussion of just what happened on the ship of abduction. The varying opinions are summed up in the figure of the goddess, Iris, who descends into their midst with messages from Aphrodite, Athena, and Zeus, all contradictory on what Paris and Helen should do.

The last major scene of the play depicts Ulysses and Hector debating the inevitability of the war. Ulysses remarks on how they are two great leaders witnessing a catastrophe from a terrace (Fry 67, Giraudoux 120).[11] But just as the two commanders are about to agree on the return of Helen, foolishness overwhelms the terrace.[12] Demokos berates Hector for negotiating the return of Helen; he won't have his war song. In a sudden rage, Hector hurls his javelin at Demokos. In his dying words, however, the persistent Demokos blames Ajax for his death. The Gates of War slowly open, revealing Helen kissing Troilus.

Oedipus, Orpheus, Odysseus—let us now have Orestes. T. S. Eliot's play of 1939, *The Family Reunion*, is the first of several plays by Eliot that have their roots in Greek myth (I omit the sketch *Sweeney Agonistes*, 1932). *The Family Reunion* by intention is a modern retelling of the Orestes myth, whereas the antique counterparts of *The Cocktail Party* (Euripides' *Alcestis*), *The Elder Statesman* (Sophocles' *Oedipus at Colonus*), and *The Confidential Clerk* (Euripides' *Ion*) are not at all obvious. To go, in time, from Gide to Eliot, as we have in this essay, is to go from the re-creation of an ancient drama to the conversion of an ancient myth into completely modern terms. The five plays have in common the use of modern diction—plain, not elaborate, the speech of ordinary, however educated, adults.[13] The characters in all of these plays are so fashioned that we the modern viewers can readily identify with them. They are part of our time. Eliot, I believe, goes the farthest in making his characters as natural and contemporary as possible.

The action of Eliot's play follows quite closely the plot
of Aeschylus's second play in *The Oresteia, The Libation
Bearers (Choephori).*[14] The main subject of the play is the
return home, to the country house, Wishwood, of its owner,
Harry, Lord Monchensey (Orestes). He is accompanied by
his loyal chauffeur, Downing (Pylades). Harry's widowed
mother, Amy (Clytemnestra), has presided over Wishwood
in his absence. (Before Harry came into his majority, Wishwood was hers.) Frail and unwell as she has been, Amy is
glad to have Harry home. The occasion is Amy's birthday,
and also present are Amy's three sisters, Ivy, Violet, and
Agatha. As a trio these women do not have a parallel in
Aeschylus, although Agatha as the resented sister of Amy
(CPP 282) can be taken as Eliot's Electra. Amy's two vapid
brothers-in-law, Gerald and Charles Piper, together supply
the Aegisthus figure. Eliot very cleverly gives us Apollo in the
person of the physician, Dr. Warburton. There is one other
character (apart from Denman, the maid): Mary, a distant
cousin of Amy. Mary has qualities of Cassandra. The Eumenides are Harry's troubled conscience, and themselves.[15]

As the play opens, the family are gathered about Amy for
sherry and cocktails. Harry is expected momentarily. Agatha
wonders whether Harry will still find Wishwood *home,* and
whether he will find his boyhood (CPP 229). At this point the
play becomes a treatment of homecoming, thus augmenting
the original Aeschylean situation.[16] The family take up the
matter of the recent death of Harry's wife during their travels, the wife for whom Amy had had little use (CPP 230).

Suddenly Harry arrives. To his family's amazement he
thinks he is being followed and watched. Harry goes on to
elaborate on his melancholy and feelings of guilt. Agatha
alone seems to be understanding and sympathetic (CPP 234–

35). It would appear that Harry pushed his wife overboard the ship on which they were sailing (CPP 235), but the death was ruled an accident. Amy thinks that a hot bath and a good dinner will help her son. Charles and the others query Downing about what happened on the ship. At Downing's departure, Charles, Gerald, Ivy, and Violet become a chorus, remarking on the instability of life (CPP 242–43). We next learn that Amy had intended Mary to be Harry's wife. Because of this disagreement, only Agatha attended Harry's wedding (CPP 245). Harry and Mary have their reunion and it is in this scene that Mary, long at Wishwood and quite subject to Amy, also takes on the qualities of an Electra. Mary reminds Harry of their happy childhood. But this fleeting moment of happiness in recollection passes, as Harry once again sees the Eumenides (CPP 252–53).

Part 2 of the play follows dinner. Dr. Warburton advises Harry that Amy has a serious heart condition; a sudden shock could kill her. Amy, meanwhile, wants Harry to assume command of Wishwood (CPP 261). As the drama continues, there is great concern for the accident Harry's brother John has suffered on his way to the reunion. Soon thereafter the family learns of the midday accident of Harry's other brother, Arthur. The family forms a chorus, and it is in this speech that the play becomes symbolic and universal, especially with the telling verses

And whether in Argos or England
There are certain inflexible laws
Unalterable, in the nature of music.
(CPP 271)

It is this allusion, this reference, that makes the play a statement of vital, general interest. Families have always been like this, before the House of Atreus and since then. The mythological image focuses and generalizes. It gives accent and distinction to an otherwise average and unexceptional situation. Eliot furthermore imbues his characters with the same natural speech that his French contemporaries display.[17] It is with this note of both distinction and broad general reference that the average and typical become eternal verity.

Harry slowly begins to make up his mind to leave Wishwood. Agatha reveals to him the old bad relations between his father and mother (CPP 274). Harry and Agatha become very close, their conversation resembling the important exchange between Orestes and Electra in the *Choephori* (Aeschylus, *Choephori* 212–63; CPP 276–81). Harry resolves to leave, to find a life of cleansing and atonement, just as Orestes goes to Delphi and Athens in search of purification in the concluding drama of *The Oresteia, The Eumenides* (CPP 281).

The family, then, is appalled to realize that Harry is really leaving. Mary and Agatha, together very much as Cassandra now, know that Harry must push on (CPP 285). It is implied that both women know of Harry's Eumenides, whether or not they have actually seen them. Amy finds herself abandoned. Harry speaks of becoming a missionary (CPP 286), while Downing observes that, as Pylades to Orestes, Lord Monchensey will not have much further need of him. A moment later, Amy is dead (CPP 290). The choral ending of the play is spoken by Mary and Agatha in terms of expiation and pilgrimage.

The virtue of the five works chosen for this essay is that, although derivative, they have an independent strength and make modern statements. *The Family Reunion* is an engrossing recasting of the Orestes story. Although less ambitious than Eugene O'Neill's *Oresteia* of 1931, *Mourning Becomes Electra*, Eliot's play has quick, light movement. O'Neill's work is ponderous, in every way lacking Eliot's lyricism. As suggested in the Introduction, I believe that many admirers of the theater would rather see a good modern production of Aeschylus's *Oresteia* than to sit through an evening of *Mourning Becomes Electra*. Likewise, there is a brilliant originality in Giraudoux's *Tiger at the Gates*. The Homeric situation and characters on the eve of war speak to us with a vital immediacy. In contrast, his *Amphitryon 38*, although possessing a bright charm, does not, I think, adapt or recast the Plautine original with sufficient originality to make it a modern classic. The vitality of the classical tradition today depends on the relationship of the modern telling of the classical theme to the artistic and social conditions of our time.[18]

A deeper question, however, remains. What was the attraction of classical myth for these playwrights? And, what was the charm of the plays for the audiences in Paris, London, and New York?

Part of the attraction is the thinly veiled sexuality of the pieces by Gide, Cocteau, and Giraudoux. The sexuality smolders in the Oedipal family as created by Gide; Cocteau's Jocasta in her delight in beautiful men anticipates the character of Norma Desmond in the later film *Sunset Boulevard* (1950). Giraudoux's Helen foreshadows the many luscious, flirtatious characters portrayed by Marilyn Monroe. The world was ready for a greater candor in the artistic presentation of the relations of the sexes, but it would be 1947 when Tennessee Williams opened the door with his brilliant and provocative *A Streetcar Named Desire*.

The French plays are also part and parcel of twentieth-century surrealism. Classical mythology is much concerned with the life and world of dreams. (The great set piece of the dream world in classical literature is the descent of Vergil's Aeneas into the underworld, *Aeneid* 6.) In *The Infernal Machine* the opening scene on the battlements, the ensuing scene with the Sphinx, and the bedroom scene all have a remote, ethereal quality, combined with a sense of the ominous, the very mood of the surrealist paintings of Giorgio de Chirico. Gide's Oedipus has a similar otherworldly quality. And would not the *Guernica* itself make a commanding backdrop for *Tiger at the Gates*?

Classical themes fitted very well with the artistic ambience, or tone, of the 1930s and served the audiences of that period with as much provocative entertainment as did mythology used by the great playwrights of the fifth century B.C. In that Greek world, so thickly adorned with mythological sculpture and painting, nobody was ignorant of the worlds of Homer and Hesiod. Everybody knew Achilles' story, and the history of Pandora. The challenge to the Greek playwright was in interpretation. His subjects were a donnée. The audience was looking for fresh twists of plot—variations in story line were admired—and splendor of language. The audiences of the 1930s were people who knew mythology fairly well through their earlier studies of Greek or Latin, or both. These modern versions of classical myth and legend were thoroughly congenial to an audience born before World War I.

Eliot is the great borrower and synthetist. His *Family Reunion* in its contemporary language, as already suggested, has a tone not dissimilar to that of Cocteau's *La Machine infernale*. Cocteau, however, kept his presentation semiantique and romantic, its settings and costumes the dreamworld of a Graustark or Zenda. Eliot does put his family in a handsome setting, the manor house of Wishwood, but otherwise his characters and their speech have the educated manner and tone of people of the upper middle class anywhere.

Eliot's play has two special distinctions. First, his source is the grandest theater piece extant from classical Greece, Aeschylus's *Oresteia*. This source immediately gives a monumentality to Eliot's work (Eliot may, indeed, go too far in his rather heavy and obvious use of the Eumenides themselves). Second, the pains and travail of modern life enunciated in the play recall themes from his early masterpiece, *The Waste Land* (1922). Amy is a latter-day Belladonna, the woman in "A Game of Chess." Harry is the embodiment of the unseen narrator in *The Waste Land*, whether one takes that narrator as Teiresias or Modern Man.

The Family Reunion, in my opinion, is more majestic than the French plays, and more solemn in meaning. But then, Eliot is the author not only of the earlier *The Waste Land* but also of *Murder in the Cathedral* (1935). The darker quality of his classical drama suits well the darkening of Europe in 1939. Humanity was less doomed—or did not see its doom—when in the late 1920s and into the 1930s the French writers produced their plays. Marguerite Yourcenar has commented (in the preface to *Feux*, discussed in a subsequent chapter) on the fascination with the film and music hall held by people in the 1930s. Certainly Gide and Cocteau offer Oedipus in rapid scenes resembling a film or ballet. *Tiger at the Gates* has a light operatic quality. Eliot's play, however, gives us a modern setting combined with a Sophoclean solemnity. His play is at once new and old.

In conclusion, the five plays under consideration offer varied approaches to the modern version of a Greek original. *La*

Machine infernale in its opening, which combines Shakespeare and Sophocles, unfolds as a glittering pastiche of ancient and modern elements. Gide's *Oedipe* buoyantly shows the banter of family life. Cocteau's *Orphée* is a balletic retelling in completely modern terms of Vergil's and Ovid's tale. Giraudoux with grace and theatrical elegance conjures up great Troy just as the volcano of World War II began to emerge. Eliot examines life on truly the eve of that conflagration. In the work of these playwrights, the myth and theater of fifth-century Greece illumine our world "between two wars."

CHAPTER FOUR

Art and Power:
Hermann Broch's
The Death of Vergil

B roch's novel dealing with the last twenty-four hours in the life of Vergil[1] is one of the great experiments in twentieth-century writing, with qualities of a majestic tone poem by Jan Sibelius or Richard Strauss.[2] In its length, complexity, and profound thought the novel is comparable to the *Aeneid*, which Broch celebrates by many references and significant quotations. The novel in the original German is a display piece of diction and style, the use of rich compound verbs and nouns making a dense verbal texture. When the 1983 reprint of Jean Starr Untermeyer's 1945 English translation of the novel was reviewed by Michael Ratcliffe in the *London Times* (28 July 1983), the review had the title "Word Storm." This apt description of the Broch novel itself is brilliantly caught by the Untermeyer translation.

The novel has three principal subjects: Vergil's reveries, often delirious, as he lies dying at Brundisium; his final interview with Caesar Augustus; his conversations with his literary executors, Plotius Tucca and Lucius Varius. These three subjects are, however, only the points of a triangle. The sides of the triangle are as complex as the ropes on the ship that carries Vergil from Greece to Italy, and the field within the triangle is as complexly wrought, filled with figures and design, as a painting by Hieronymus Bosch or Jackson Pollock.

The circumstances of Vergil's death at Brundisium are well known.[3] In 19 B.C. the poet had taken himself to Greece to study and to enjoy a change from the labors of his *Aeneid,* on which he had been working for some twelve years. His plans were interrupted when he met Augustus in Athens and Augustus persuaded Vergil to return to Italy with him. Unfortunately, Vergil fell ill at Megara and returned to Italy only to die at the port of entry, Brundisium. Although the *Aeneid* was incomplete, with several finishing touches needed, Augustus had the poem published soon after the poet's death. Against this simple background and working with the three principal circumstances of Vergil's mental state and the two lengthy conversations, Hermann Broch created a monument for our time. Embraced by the three fundamental elements in the novel are the following major themes: the tortured artist in a miserable world; the unity of earth and the cosmos as expressed by song and sound; the nature of love and beauty; the relationship between the *Aeneid* and Caesar Augustus. Strong subordinate themes are the significance of Vergil's Mantuan boyhood and youth and his relationship with the woman Plotia Hieria, a relationship just mentioned in the biography by Donatus. All of these themes, principal and subordinate, are related, are interlocking, and are mutually reflective.

Broch's Vergil feels that he has lived a driven life, that he has been a lodger in his own life, thus very much the isolated outsider (Untermeyer 13, Broch 13). This loneliness has two aspects: the artist has been thrown by fate into the "prison of art" (Untermeyer 137, Broch 130), and at the same time the artist is tempted to be fascinated by his own "godlikeness" in his "dalliance with beauty" (Untermeyer 141, Broch 134). The reader is reminded of Gustav von Aschen-

bach in Mann's *Death in Venice*.[4] Vergil condemns himself
for not succeeding in depicting real human beings in the
Aeneid (Untermeyer 152, Broch 145–46) as well as for not
offering real help to the human community (Untermeyer
143, Broch 137). At the same time, Broch's Vergil perceives
the challenge of art, or art's despair:

> its despairing attempt
> to build up the imperishable from things that perish,
> from words, from sounds, from stones, from colors,
> so that space, being formed,
> might outlast time.
>
> (Untermeyer 122, Broch 116)[5]

It is, however, the arrival at his sickbed of Plotius Tucca and
Lucius Varius which brings Vergil to the nadir of his self-
scorn and self-condemnation. These friends are typical visitors to the sickroom, exuding as they do optimism for the
ailing poet and assurance of his steady improvement. To
Tucca and Varius Vergil expresses his desire to burn the
Aeneid (Untermeyer 239, Broch 224–25).[6] Shocked by the
very idea, the two friends strongly resist the notion and pro-
ceed to extol Vergil's accomplishments. They remark on him
as a master along with Lucretius, Catullus, Propertius, and
Tibullus. Vergil observes that the younger poets had the ben-
efit of dying young and probably were more honest in their
art than he has been. Lucius contradicts Vergil's opinion, to
which Vergil replies, "The question of honesty and dishon-
esty is no longer an artistic question: the aim is toward the
essential in human life before which art is almost negligible,
since it is able to express only the human element" (Untermeyer 253, Broch 238).

As Broch's Vergil condemns his artistry, he also muses

over and hymns the forces of love and beauty, both of which he feels he has known more as an observer than as a participant. As Vergil lies there so alone in Brundisium, his delirious mind conjures up for him recollections of two lovers, both mentioned in the ancient biographies: a woman, Plotia Hieria, and a boy, Alexis.[7] He remembers the day when he read aloud to Plotia the Fourth Eclogue, for the writing of which the beautiful Plotia had been the inspiration (Untermeyer 65, Broch 64). When, however, Vergil converses with his executors, he remarks on how the Fourth Eclogue had been a poem of thanks to Asinius Pollio, who had given him the boy Alexis (Untermeyer 251, Broch 236). Broch sees the Fourth Eclogue as a hymn to womanhood and motherhood; the wonderful child of the poem is realized in Alexis.

Yet Broch's Vergil feels unsatisfied. At the height of his delirium (which condition dominates the long second section of the novel, "Fire—The Descent"), a voice cries out to him, "Open your eyes to love!" (Untermeyer 221, Broch 210). While he is is conversing with Plotius and Tucca, half listening, half in revery, a statement comes to Vergil's mind: "Love is the reality" (Untermeyer 250, Broch 235). It is Vergil's growing sense of the permanent, all-embracing presence of Love in the universe that makes him respond to humanity in his last few hours, and so he accedes to Augustus's request that the *Aeneid* be surrendered to him.

In the meantime, however, Broch's Vergil is enmeshed in a revery on the nature of earthly love. Like his character Aeneas, Vergil has been in flight from love. Aeneas had forsaken Dido, and Broch's Vergil finds himself very like Aeneas (Untermeyer 66, Broch 64). Yet Vergil cannot get Plotia out of his mind. In a fresh revery following the visit of the physician, Charondas, Vergil sees Plotia stepping out of a tree trunk

(Untermeyer 292, Broch 274) and to her Vergil says, "I love you." "I love you," is the reply (Untermeyer 298, Broch 279). Yet immediately Vergil's mind goes back to Dido and Aeneas, and the vision is clouded by the appearance of a harsh Fama (Untermeyer 302, Broch 283). Broch's Vergil feels that he has been denied the reality of love, thus his poetry is marked by a hollowness (Untermeyer 275, Broch 241–42). Catullus, Tibullus, and Propertius had been granted the power to love, "and from love they had derived a premonition of reality which was stronger than any harmony and passed earthly things" (Untermeyer 257, Broch 242).

As Broch's Vergil feels that he has known too little of love, so he laments his "dalliance with beauty" (Untermeyer 141, Broch 134). He has been too sophisticated, too mannered in his art. In fact, he muses, "knowledge of beauty was lack of knowledge, perception of beauty was lack of perception" (Untermeyer 119, Broch 113).

In his delirium Broch's Vergil suddenly realizes that beauty can be broken, destroyed, annihilated. The destroyer is laughter (Untermeyer 126, Broch 120). In the hymn which follows this revelation, Vergil hears these lines:

and though it were Zeus who struck up laughter in the circle
of the male gods,
it was the human being who aroused the laughter of the gods.
(Untermeyer 127, Broch 121)[8]

As the artist dallies with beauty, and in his isolation begins to perceive his own "god-likeness" (Untermeyer 141, Broch 134), he is only an object of mockery to the gods. Vergil continues later in the novel to have only disparagement for himself: "he the mere word-maker who must needs destroy his work because the humane, the round of human action and the human need for help, had meant so little to him that everything which he should have retained and depicted in love was never written down, but simply and uselessly transfigured and magnified to beauty" (Untermeyer 225–26, Broch 214).

The artist, his world, the presence in both art and life of love and beauty—these great themes in Broch's novel are held together by the chain, the cord of the *Aeneid*. The scrolls of the masterpiece are constantly at Vergil's side on board the ship, in the litter that bears Vergil to the imperial residence at Brundisium, and in his room in the palace. The great debate in the mind of Broch's Vergil, as he lies there dying, is whether to destroy the masterwork, filled with as much falseness and imperfection as Vergil believes there is in the poem.

Broch's treatment of the *Aeneid* takes the form of paraphrase and direct translation from the Latin. The passages are in the mind of Vergil or are recited. The major citations are from book 6 (the mysteries of life) and book 8 (the grandeur of Rome), with some reference as cited above to Dido in book 4, and to Turnus in book 12.[9] Although Broch's Vergil discredits all of his work "from the Aetna Song to the Aeneid" (Untermeyer 142, Broch 135),[10] Broch clearly has only admiration for Vergil's *Aeneid,* even for the famous incomplete half-lines ("waiting-stones"—Untermeyer 430, Broch 407).

Ever concerned with his burden and his plight as an artist, Broch's Vergil sees himself in a descent into hell, and in his delirium expresses a fine translation of *Aeneid* 6.126–52, "facilis descensus Averno" (Untermeyer 137–38, Broch 131). Later, in an apostrophe to Plotia, Vergil recalls the idea of a descent to the underworld and wishes that he could return by the Gate of Horn (not the Gate of Ivory, by which Aeneas returns). The Gate of Horn gives access to true knowledge.

Soon thereafter Vergil is encouraged. In his delirium since he was carried off the ship he has been alert to a guide, a companion. This boy is named Lysanias, and he comforts the great Vergil in his illness. When Broch's Vergil announces his plan to burn the *Aeneid* (Untermeyer 188, Broch 180), Lysanias is horrified. Thereupon follows a scene (Untermeyer 192–95, Broch 183–85) in which Lysanias reads at length from *Aeneid* 8.310–69. It is old Italy, of which Vergil is a master, and Aeneas traversing the site of future Rome. The reading of this passage gives Vergil some peace, some rest.

In his visit with the poet, Caesar Augustus has the *Aeneid* much in mind. The *princeps* also singles out the Shield passage in *Aeneid* 8 for special praise because the lines depict so well the victory at Actium (Untermeyer 305, Broch 286). Augustus prevails upon Vergil to recite aloud lines 675–88, wherein Octavian Caesar stands on his victorious ship in the waters of Actium. (Untermeyer misreads *actische* for *Attic*). Pleased with the recitation, Augustus associates the triumphal lines with the fact that his birthday is on the morrow. Later in this conversation, as Vergil belittles his accomplishment, Augustus firmly declares to him: "It is no longer your work, it is the work of all of us, indeed in one sense we have all labored at it, and finally it is the creation of the Roman people and their greatness" (Untermeyer 313, Broch 293–94). And then Augustus himself, displaying his own command of Vergil's poem, recites the *excudent alii* passage from book 6 (847–53), ending with the remark, "Well, Virgil, are you caught in your own net?" (Untermeyer 314, Broch 294). To which Vergil replies, "Caesar, my work remains undone, terrifyingly undone, and nobody wants to believe me in this!" (Untermeyer 315, Broch 295).

In the end, Vergil gives the *Aeneid* to Augustus. Lysanias reappears, coming before Augustus as an acolyte to a shrine

(Untermeyer 393, Broch 371). Lysanias, in greeting, chants the panegyric to Augustus from book 6.789–800. In this moment of high art and highest imperial sentiment, Vergil presents the poem to Caesar Augustus (Untermeyer 394, Broch 371–72).

Broch's Augustus captures well the ever-young monarch of the many portraits as well as the man of steel whom we know from history. From the moment he enters the room of the dying Vergil, Broch's Augustus is majestic, gracious, alternatively humorous and grave, devoted to Vergil, and certain of the greatness of Vergil's poetry. Broch is clear in his admiration of Caesar Augustus, frequently employing such descriptive terms as "the consecrated person" and "the sacred one" (*geheiligte, Geheiligten;* Untermeyer 303, Broch 284). The interview between Vergil and Augustus, their last conversation, is given a cosmic proportion in that a slight earthquake takes place simultaneously (Untermeyer 320–21, Broch 300–301).

It is Augustus's task to cause Vergil to part freely with the poem. Their conversation veers and sways like the lamp in the earth tremor, as slowly, slowly Augustus brings Vergil around to his point of view (the conversation takes up pages 303–98 in the Untermeyer translation, pages 284–376 in the Suhrkamp German edition).

Broch's Augustus conforms well to the complex portrait given by Suetonius in his biography, to the great statesman whose words are engraved in the *Res Gestae,* and to the picture offered by Ronald Syme in his influential work of 1939, *The Roman Revolution.* Syme's Octavian–Caesar Augustus is the gifted opportunist, a man with a sense of destiny, a monarch of monarchs. In Broch's novel Caesar Augustus has one diplomatic task: to make Vergil want to surrender to him and to the Roman world his masterpiece, the *Aeneid,* however flawed its author believes it to be. Augustus succeeds in this mission. As the interview comes to its end, the poet and the emperor exchange benedictions. Vergil: "Accept my thanks for so many things." Augustus: "My thanks go to you, Virgil." And as Augustus leaves Vergil for the last time, he turns to say: "May your eyes rest on me always, my Virgil" (Untermeyer 398, Broch 375–76).

The very end of the interview takes a twist, as Caesar Augustus finally leaves the chamber. "Caesar, svelte, proud and masterful; at his heels a tawny lion, which followed the casket with steps heavy and slow, and many of those present joined in the procession" (Untermeyer 398, Broch 376). This is truly Symes's Caesar Augustus. He is both the lord of the *Res Gestae* and the presiding genius of the Ara Pacis.[11]

In the remaining pages of the novel Broch's Vergil slips in and out of delirium. He is able to focus on one important matter, his will. In the meantime, he has seen his own supreme talisman, the Golden Bough (Untermeyer 426, Broch 402). With the completion of the will (Untermeyer 433–35, Broch 409–12), Vergil makes ready for a new existence. Part 4 of Broch's novel has the title "Air—The Homecoming."

After the dictation of his will to Plotius and Lucius, Vergil thinks he is in a rowboat at sea (Untermeyer 440, Broch 414). He leaves Horace and Propertius standing on the shore in an attitude of friendly farewell. Thereupon his vessel is joined by other ethereal vessels bearing Tibullus, Lucretius, Sallust, and Varro (Untermeyer 443, Broch 417). "Stillness within stillness" (Untermeyer 444, Broch 418), the world of water mingles with the hush awaiting a lyre-singer, who will strike a "spheric song" (Untermeyer 445, Broch 419). Throughout the book Broch's Vergil is alert to the presence of Earth, the presence of Life within the cosmos. The essence of the cosmos is expressive song and sound. Thus, here near the end, Vergil is remarkably attuned to the musical oneness of life and the cosmos. He envisions a paradise of animals as he, and Plotia, too, are carried into a Garden of Eden where everything is magnificently pristine (Untermeyer 458–62, Broch 432–36). At last Vergil perceives a human face, "and this face could be beheld in the middle of the world-shield, in its infinite depth, beheld there amidst infinite human life and human living" (Untermeyer 480, Broch 452). Broch thus sums up the message of Anchises in book 6 of the *Aeneid,* and the significance of Aeneas's shield in book 8. The world is one world, the world of Rome was One World.

The ending of Broch's novel is inimitable, beyond paraphrase. It sums up Vergil's work and his achievement:

> The word hovered over the universe, over the nothing, floating beyond the expressible as well as the inexpressible, and he, caught under and amidst the roaring, he floated on with the word, although the more he was enveloped by it, the more he penetrated into the flooding sound and was penetrated by it, the more unattainable, the greater, the graver and more elusive became the word, a floating sea, a floating fire, sea-heavy, sea-light, notwithstanding it was still the word: he could not hold fast to it and he might not hold fast to it; incomprehensible and unutterable for him: it was the word beyond speech.
>
> (Untermeyer 481–82, Broch 454)

A comparative word, however, needs to be said in conclusion. Two questions come to the reader: Is Broch's novel comparable to the *Aeneid* itself? Is Broch's Vergil one of the memorable creations, characterizations of our time? Broch himself saw his work as epic in scope (Broch 490), yet was striving more for lyrical expression (Broch 458, 462). In this regard Broch never saw his work as a Joycean *Ulysses* either in scope or in technique (Broch 458, 491). As mentioned at the beginning of this essay, a musical analogy is more descriptive of Broch's work, an analogy much supported by Broch in his commentary (see my note 2). In its minute and intense presentation of a man's thoughts at a critical juncture in his life, the novel has a certain epic quality. If, however, epic is characterized by range and variety of action performed by several characters in positive and negative relationships, and I think this is a description of ancient epic, then *The Death of Vergil* is not an epic, nor was it meant to be. Broch's novel, therefore, is in no sense an imitation of an antique work. It is a work of modern art, not a modern *Aeneid*.

Broch's Vergil is, however, as fascinating and memorable (if not haunting) a characterization as the other wonderful fictional creations of our time. This Vergil is on a par with Mann's von Aschenbach, with Yourcenar's Hadrian, with Eliot's Harry, Lord Monchensey, with Aiken's Mr. Arcularis. If he is not so many-faceted as Mann's Adrian Leverkühn (*Doctor Faustus*), to my mind the supreme fictional creation of the century, it is because Broch was not writing that kind of a novel and his subject, although complex enough as an artist and a human being, if the ancient lives mean anything at all, not to mention the man behind the poetry, was not quite so tormented and driven a person as Mann's composer. Broch's novel strove for the word beyond speech. Nevertheless, Broch's Vergil is one of the masterful portraits in twentieth-century art.

CHAPTER FIVE

Changing Visions:
Three American Poets
in Italy

The attraction of Italy—Venice, Florence, and Rome, in particular—for American writers and artists in the nineteenth and early twentieth centuries is well known. The works of Hawthorne, James, and Wharton are saturated with the Italian landscape, especially the cityscape of the three great cities mentioned. During the second half of the nineteenth century, Paris began to offer the lure of modern art because of the preeminence of French painting in the art world. American artists of every art form had their time in Paris, the whole experience being summed up in the famous home and salon of Gertrude Stein and her relatives. Artists still traveled in Italy, but more for the charm of it all. The avantgarde was in Paris, to a lesser degree in London, although it could be observed that Virginia Woolf and her brilliant circle were the earlier and then contemporary British counterpart of Gertrude Stein and her remarkable friends. Italy still provided stimulus, however, as is seen in the career of Pablo Picasso, whose visits in 1917 to Rome and Pompeii made a major impact on that artist and inspired the many classical figures and themes in his work of the 1920s and early 1930s.

It was after World War II that Rome again became a magnet for Americans. Rome of the Via Veneto is etched vividly in Tennessee Williams's novella of 1950, *The Roman Spring of*

Mrs. Stone. Rome and southern Italy, the Amalfi coast especially, are the rich backdrop for William Styron's powerful novel of 1960, *Set This House on Fire.*

Our concern in this study, however, is with poetry and the classical world. Our interest is in the reflection of classical settings, and classical concepts as related to the settings, in the work of three poets who have visited Italy.[1] Professor Lillian Feder has covered the influences of classical myth on modern poetry.[2] The concern here is with the physical ancient world as it survives today and affects the modern writer.

By modern poetry, I mean the poetry of the last thirty years. I am excluding from this discussion, except for the sake of brief comparison, the poetry of the first half of the twentieth century, which was dominated by the work of Yeats, Pound, and Eliot, with Eliot being the most influential.

In 1964 Chad Walsh of Beloit College published a rich anthology which he called *Today's Poets: American and British Poetry Since the 1930's.*[3] As one goes through this collection one finds so many overtones of Eliot, in style, manner, and attitude. If you take the first of the *Four Quartets,* "Burnt Norton" (1935), as typical of Eliot's high style, where the *vates* (prophet and bard) of our century produces some of his most limpid phrases and some of his most arresting incantations, then many poems of the mid-century poets are found to be very "Eliotesque." Consider such lines from "Burnt Norton" as

Time and the bell have buried the day,
The black cloud carries the sun away.
Will the sunflower turn to us, will the clematis
Stray down, bend to us.[4]

And compare such passages as Theodore Roethke, "The Far Field":

> The river turns on itself,
> The tree retreats into its own shadow
> I feel a weightless change, a moving forward.[5]

William Empson, "Doctrinal Point":

> The god approached dissolves into the air.
>
> Magnolias, for instance, when in bud,
> Are right in doing anything they can think of;
> Free by predestination in the blood.[6]

W. D. Snodgrass, "The Operation":

> Into flowers, into women, I have awakened.
> Too weak to think of strength, I have thought all day,
> Or dozed among standing friends, I lie in night, now.
> A small mound under linen like the drifted snow.
> Only by nurses visited, in radiance, saying, Rest.[7]

Eliot's example was, in certain respects, a very good one. His forte is his lyricism combined with a straightforward vocabulary, one that avoids rare or pompous words. Some of Eliot's greatest strokes are achieved with the simplest English, and I quote again from "Burnt Norton":

> Footfalls echo in the memory
> Down the passage which we did not take
> Towards the door we never opened
> Into the rose-garden.[8]

On the other hand, in his masterpiece the *Four Quartets*, in this major poem, there are only four specific classical allusions; none at all in the last quartet, "Little Gidding."[9] The author of the Sweeney poems with their many references to classical literature and mythology; the erudite poet of *The Waste Land*, full of classical allusions and of such a nature that Northrop Frye was moved to call it "an intensely Latin poem";[10] the playwright who brought the House of Atreus into his *Family Reunion*—our archpoet in his last great poem nearly abandoned classical antiquity! In "Burnt Norton" there are the two epigraphs from Heracleitos and a reference to "the loud lament of the disconsolate chimera." In the third quartet, "The Dry Salvages," we read at one point, "And the way up is the way down, the way forward is the way back," an echo of the epigraph to "Burnt Norton." "The Dry Salvages" was written in 1940–41. In "Little Gidding" there is nothing. In "East Coker" we do have lines which remind us of Aratus, Vergil, and Ovid:

Thunder rolled by the rolling stars
Simulates triumphal cars
Deployed in constellated wars
Scorpion fights against the Sun.[11]

The imagery is that of Vergil in *Georgics* 1.34–35. But at the end of this passage we can only have a sinking feeling when our poet, president in 1944 of the Virgil Society of England, declares:

That was a way of putting it—not very satisfactory:
A periphrastic study in a worn-out poetical fashion.[12]

The greatest scholar-poet of our age is disgusted with classical allusion. Perhaps in 1941 he was beginning to be weary of making poems that would have little meaning for most readers. That is, by 1941, in the middle, for England, of World War II, a *vates* like Eliot just possibly could see to our day, when a classical education is the exception and not the rule: when, in fact, education has become so varied and departmentalized that we cannot count on anything being common knowledge.

The year 1950 then, is a real turning point in the progress of English and American poetry. By that time the foremost poet of England and America had turned away from classical influences, and many younger poets were turning away both from classical influences, and from T. S. Eliot. (The *new* leading figure is yet to be identified; the poets of very recent times are extremely diverse.) On the other hand, beginning about 1950, by which time affairs in Europe had become fairly stable again, we do find references to classical antiquity returning to poetry. The cause was travel.

Three poets whose work, I feel, is representative of recent serious American poetry are Frederick Nicklaus, James Dickey, and Richard Wilbur.

Now when James Dickey, Frederick Nicklaus, and Richard Wilbur went to the Mediterranean, and to Italy, they were not utterly unprepared. They did not bring to the classical lands the highly prepared reactions that Eliot would have offered. Nor in these poets was there such a "shock of recognition"[13] that they wanted to sit down at once and write a poem on a classical subject. Poets certainly have reacted to antiquity that spontaneously. Cavafy is an obvious example with such poems as "Orophernes," which begins

> He who here upon the tetradrachm
> appears to have a smiling face,
> the handsome, delicate face
> he is Orophernes, son of Ariarathes.[14]

So, too, Lawrence Durrell, with his "Orpheus," "Patmos," "At Epidauros," "To Argo," "Penelope," and "Daphnis and

Chloe." Cavafy, of course, is an older poet. Born in 1863 and dying in 1933, Cavafy is of the age of Yeats but is akin in spirit to Swinburne and Oscar Wilde. Durrell is a modern. His first poems appeared in 1943. The trouble with Durrell is that he does not have much to say, at least to me, and his classical references are more decorative than meaningful.

The three poets we are considering then, all good poets, went to Europe. They brought to their experience great perception, if not Alexandrian erudition. They were not over-awed by classical antiquity but intuitively appreciated its special significance and then related it to their world, our world now. All three of these poets were affected by the spectacle of ancient Greece and Rome, and in the reactions of all them there is the feeling of Keats himself when he first saw the Parthenon sculptures and could only feel

> a dizzy pain,
> That mingles Grecian grandeur with the rude
> Wasting of old Time—with a billowy main,
> A sun, a shadow of a magnitude.
> ("On Seeing the Elgin Marbles
> for the First Time")

Frederick Nicklaus began his travels in the early 1960s. At first he concentrated on northern and central Europe, as is reflected in his poems, which were collected under the title *The Man Who Bit the Sun* and published by New Directions in 1964. Then came a major journey to the Mediterranean, which centered on Sicily and southern Italy. His discovery of southern Europe was a deep experience, although at first he was simply impressed by the panorama itself. This experience is reflected in his second book, *Cut of Noon*, published in 1971. Here is "Leopardi":

The thing I noticed first was not the room
itself, its view of sea and cliffs contained
within deep arches, nor its shadowed cool
of tiles and plaster walls, but *Leopardi*
spelled on the blackest book spine, leaning toward me.

So he has stalked me even to this town
above the pleasure coast that runs away
from Naples killing with its cholera,
the coast where even to pronounce it—death—
becomes an obscene rasping of the breath.

Ignoring him, and Naples, and the dead
volcano's peak, not hearing after dark
the rats that run along the trellis tops,
half-blinded by the day's prismatic light,
I will forget him and his horrible night.

He waits me though, in sound of surf that crumbles
shoreward, and softly as volcanic ash
half parts my sleeper's lips, and calls in wind
that wakes me to the darkness and myself.
Then I take Leopardi from the shelf

and read him on the balcony, the lamp-
thrown shadows twisted as his back, until
far at the farthest angle of my view
Naples emerges, gray and filmy shape,
the dread miasma I shall not escape.

Once more I pack to leave a paradise,
pay up the bill and tip the porters, start
back down the sunny road that brought me here,
my life once more his night of Recanati,
the dark within me that I cannot flee.[15]

The general setting of this narrative poem is that of the
Amalfi Drive, running from Sorrento to Salerno. The towns

along or above the drive—Positano, Amalfi, Ravello—make up one of the most beautiful resorts in the world. The narrator, however, is alert to the contrast between life on this pleasure coast and the life of the moldering harbor city of Naples, on the other side of the Lattari Mountains from the Amalfi coast. The narrator thinks also of the famous Mount Vesuvius, ever looming over the Bay of Naples, and its destructive eruptions. In his concentrated reflection on the locale he has left, or the locale behind him, the narrator almost can see Naples, as a phantom, a haunting "gray and filmy shape."

Then, Leopardi, the great nineteenth-century Italian poet, born at Recanati, who as a youth had mastery of Greek and Latin and as a young man wrote a commentary on Plotinus. Despite poverty and poor health, Leopardi wrote lyric poems which, collected under the title *I Canti,* are among the finest in European literature. He spent his last years in despondence in Naples, where he died at the age of thirty-nine.

In this poem Nicklaus blends Recanati and Naples, the towns of Leopardi's birth and death. The two old cities, the volcano that ruined the Sorrento peninsula in the eruption of 24 August 79 A.D., are in sharp contrast to the "paradise" in which the narrator muses. The sadness of life that Leopardi knew is more typical of the human condition than the fleeting days of pleasure that the visitor to Amalfi enjoys. The creative artist, however, leaves behind work, which outlives down the ages the volcanic ash of human sadness.

In "Balloon" Nicklaus gives us Rome of the High Renaissance and Saint Peter's:

All else must fade, this city and its dome,
the dusk of balconies, wind-circling birds

above the gardens and the gardened roofs;
hushed voices, then the vast insistent moan
through squares and byways of the traffic geared
anew for night.[16]

It is the city at dusk, after siesta. The day of a beautiful afternoon, like a yellow balloon, has passed, as everything must
pass. The afternoon can, however, be remembered, and the
memory is as lasting as Saint Peter's dome, so dominant over
the cityscape of Rome.

In "The Pumice Edge,"[17] a narrative poem set in Taormina,
in Sicily, Nicklaus's view becomes both deeper and darker.
He is aware of both the futile and the tragic aspects of man's
history, of the capriciousness of fate.

After the cities and their many fountains
she brought me here, to live beneath a mountain's
anger masked with snow.

Of course it is Etna, which

mountain counts its vintages, and kills
halfway sometimes.

At the heart of the poem a man awakes beside his lover.

While she slept
again I saw us as a pair of dogs
coupled in lava for some discerning age.

The allusion is to the famous forms of plaster made by
Giuseppe Fiorelli during the excavation of Pompeii between
1860 and 1875 and on display there today. Nicklaus's
awareness of the southern Italian landscape is acute. His own
outlook was reinforced by his appreciation of the sad history

of unhappy events which have been characteristic of Sicily from the Peloponnesian War until recent times.

* * *

James Dickey found himself in Europe in 1954 and 1963 and from those experiences produced a poem worthy of the classical poems of Yates, Auden, or Millay. With Dickey we leave the general scenery of the classical lands and the general sense of the past that are characteristics of Frederick Nicklaus's "classical" poems, and focus on a specific classical locale, none other than Pompeii itself. Dickey's poem "In the Lupanar at Pompeii,"[18] is a brilliant epitome of sexual love, such as we find in Millay's sonnet "Oh, Sleep Forever in the Latmian Cave." But Dickey probes more deeply and comes up with one of the most arresting questions in twentieth-century poetry, as provocative as the questions in Yeats's famous "Leda and the Swan," and I quote from Yeats:

And how can body, laid in that white rush,
But feel the strange heart beating where it lies?

Being so caught up,
So mastered by the brute blood of the air,
Did she put on his knowledge with his power
Before the indifferent beak could let her drop?

In Dickey's poem the narrator walks the streets of the excavated city, "as tourist, but mostly as lecher." Upon reaching the lupanar

I sit down in one of the rooms
where it happened again and again.

The poet goes on to say:

I think of the marvel of lust
which can always, at any moment,
Become more than it believed,
And almost always is less:

It must be like the first
Soft floating of ash,

When in the world's frankest hands,
Someone lay with his body shaken
Free of the self: that amazement—
For we who must try to explain
Ourselves in the house of this flesh
Never can tell the quick heat
Of our own from another's breathing.

At first such calculated passion reminds us of the scene in part 3 of *The Waste Land*, where Eliot's Tiresias observes "at the violet hour" the lovemaking of the typist and her "young man carbuncular."[19] But the reader with a classical background finds himself going back to the ending of book 3 of the *Iliad*, where Paris exercises his power over Helen, or to the earlier "View from the Wall," where Helen marvels at lust and admits to Priam that she has been a slave to passion:

and I wish bitter death had been what I wanted, when I came
   hither
following your son, forsaking my chamber, my kinsmen,
my grown child, and the loveliness of girls my own age.
. . . .
. . . slut that I am. Did this ever happen?"
                         (3.173–75, 180, trans. Richmond Lattimore)

And so to my point. Unencumbered, independent of, free from erudition, the poets since 1950 when they *do* refer to antiquity take it up in grand sweeping terms that recall some

of the finest moments in the classical writers themselves;
moreover, when these newer poets are good they are very
good, and their work can be compared to the classics. Both
Nicklaus and Dickey evoke passion in a monumental setting,
such as that described by Catullus in his seventh poem,
where

> sidera multa, cum tacet nox,
> furtivos hominum vident amores

> The many stars, in the silent
> night, watch the secret love of human beings

near the

> oraclum Iovis . . . aestuosi
> et Batti veteris sacrum sepulcrum.

> oracle of tempestuous Jupiter and
> the sacred tombs of ancient Battus.

> (My translations)

Or Vergil, as he places Dido and Aeneas in a setting of regal
magnificence on the occasion of Dido's welcoming banquet:

> Postquam prima quies epulis mensaeque remotae,
> crateras magnos statuunt et uina coronant.
> fit strepitus tectis uocemque per ampla uolutant
> atria; dependent lychni laquearibus aureis
> incensi et noctem flammis funalia uincunt.
> (Aeneid 1.723–27)

> After the first respite came to the
> banqueters and the tables were removed,
> they set out great wine craters and crown
> the wine. A huzza goes up to the roof and
> they roll their voices throughout the

spacious banquet-hall; lighted chandeliers
hang down from the gilded coffering—the
candles conquer the night with their flames.
                                    (My translation)

The first-rate modern poets bring to the classical lands a
great depth of understanding. Brought up in the years of the
catastrophe of the Second World War, acutely aware of their
own time in which people hope against hope, these poet-
travelers have had an intuition which makes them see Antiquity with almost a Vergilian grasp of the whole grand and
tragic scene. Both Nicklaus and Dickey bring to the classical
lands a keen perceptiveness, the like of which is rarely
found, even in the works of the earlier twentieth-century
poets who were almost classical scholars in their own right.
The novelist Henry James had a similar understanding, and it
comes out, appropriately enough, in his essay written in
1900 on "Capri and the Bay of Naples." In this essay James
describes a visit of the preceding summer to Capri and Axel
Munthe's Villa San Michele. From a belvedere there, "the
grand air of it all was in one's very nostrils and seemed to
come from sources too numerous and too complex to name.
It was antiquity in solution." James goes on to speak of the
whole panorama as being of "extraordinary uplifted distinction," a distinction which is, however, to James, "beautiful,
horrible, and haunted," and he concludes by saying: "To
make so much distinction, how much history had been
needed!—so that the whole air still throbbed and ached
with it."[20]

James Dickey in the lupanar was acutely sensitive to the
pain of all that life, and he, like James, relates his experience
at Pompeii to life in general.

At the end of his poem Dickey very quietly says:

> We never can really tell
> Whether nature condemns us or loves us
> As we lie here dying of breath
> And the painted, unchanging women,
> Believing the desperate dead
> Where they stripped to the skin of the soul
> And whispered to us, as to
> Their panting, observing selves:
> "Passion. Before we die
> Let us hope for no longer
> But truly know it."

An awful hope, one which certainly dominated ancient writers at least as early as Plato and which is dominant in the Tenth Eclogue of Vergil, not to mention later Christian writers who explored the meaning of love and the possibility of its attainment. As T. S. Eliot says of Love in "Little Gidding" (part 4):

> Love is the unfamiliar Name
> Behind the hands that wove
> The intolerable shirt of flame
> Which human power cannot remove.
>> We only live, only suspire
>> Consumed by either fire or fire.[21]

*   *   *

And so we return to Rome.

> Under the bronze crown
> Too big for the head of the stone cherub whose feet
> A serpent has begun to eat,
> Sweet water brims a cockle and braids down
>
> Past spattered mosses, breaks
> On the tipped edge of a second shell . . .

                    . . . and makes
           A scrim or summery tent
      For a faun-ménage . . . .

. . . .
                        Yet since this all
             Is pleasure, flash, and waterfall,
      Must it not be too simple? Are we not

           More intricately expressed
      In the plain fountains that Maderna set
           Before St. Peter's . . . ?

                        . . . if those water-saints display
      The pattern of our areté,
      What of these showered fauns in this bizarre,
           Spangled, and plunging house?

These are lines from Richard Wilbur's poem "A Baroque
Wall-Fountain in the Villa Sciarra,"[22] which undoubtedly was
inspired by his term in 1954–55 at the American Academy in
Rome. The poem is collected in his 1956 volume *Things of
This World,* which includes such other poems of the Roman
scene as "Piazza di Spagna, Early Morning" and "For the
New Railway Station in Rome" with its scholarly reminis-
cence of the Servian Wall.

   The poem "A Baroque Wall-Fountain in the Villa Sciarra" takes
us from lushly carved figures of pleasure—the stone cherub, a
group of fauns, a god holding up the shell-basin—to an arresting consideration of the meaning of *areté,* (roughly, excel-
lence, both physical and mental), then on to Francis,

                    who lay in sister snow
      Before the wealthy gate.

In the work of Richard Wilbur we find a striking blending of
several aspects of the cultural history of the Western world.
In a writer like Wilbur we are reassured of the truth of T. S.

Eliot's views: "The historical sense compels a man to write not merely with his own generation in his bones, but with a feeling that the whole of the literature of Europe from Homer and within it the whole of the literature of his own country has a simultaneous existence and composes a simultaneous order."[23] In Wilbur's poem is stated the old but still arresting problem of the conflict within us of Apollonian and Dionysian elements. We can be, as Wilbur suggests,

> a clambering mesh
of water-lights . . .

. . . where ripple-shadows come
And go in swift reticulum

and rejoice like the baroque fauness in "saecular ecstasy." On the other hand, we can be straight as a line and strive ever upwards, "struggling aloft," as Wilbur describes the Maderna fountain, self-consumed by a Platonic idea, "in the act of rising." Wilbur juxtaposes the Apollonian attitude with the Dionysian, but suggests his own admiration for the latter when he speaks of the baroque statues

Reproving our disgust and our ennui
    With humble insatiety.

Nevertheless, Wilbur returns to a consideration of the dualism, the contradiction that is in human nature. And masterfully he sums it up in the figure of Saint Francis, who with extraordinary rectitude could lie in the snow, freezing and praising, at the same time attuned to a state of bliss—

That land of tolerable flowers . . .
Where eyes become the sunlight . . .
                . . . the dreamt land
Toward which all hunger leaps, all pleasures pass.

The Apollonian, the Dionysian, the Christian ideal which came from the matrix of Greece and Rome—the whole of the Western intellectual tradition, in the fullest sense of the term—is summed up in the microcosm of Wilbur's poem from the Villa Sciarra.

In poems by Frederick Nicklaus we have the panorama of the classical landscape, in particular the Bay of Naples and Vesuvius, but before that landscape is the figure of the great Italian poet of the early nineteenth century, Leopardi, lover of Greek and Latin literature, whose sense of the tragedy in life was like that of Euripides or Vergil. Nicklaus pays homage to Leopardi and to Leopardi's understanding of the human condition.

> He waits me though, in sound of surf that crumbles
> shoreward, and softly as volcanic ash
> half parts my sleeper's lips, and calls in wind
> that wakes me to the darkness and myself.
> Then I take Leopardi from the shelf
>
> and read him on the balcony, the lamp-
> thrown shadows twisted as his back, until
> far at the farthest angle of my view
> Naples emerges, gray and filmy shape,
> the dread miasma I shall not escape.

Like Henry James from the heights of Anacapri, Nicklaus with a similar sense of history came to the bay, and with Leopardi was most aware of the tears of things ("sunt lacrimae rerum," *Aeneid* 1.462).

James Dickey strolled through the provocative ruins of Pompeii and asked the perennial question: Does nature condemn us or love us? And when he concludes his poem on the lupanar with

Passion. Before we die
Let us hope for no longer
But truly know it

he is also asking how we can find meaning in life. These piercing questions, however, take on a greater depth and importance in the historical and philosophical context provided by the famous classical city which, brought back to life by excavation, has become timeless.

In Richard Wilbur's poem we have a perfect illustration of the present-day vitality of the classical tradition. The baroque sculpture with its antecedents in classical statuary; the dramatic use of the word *areté* with all its suggestions of Greek *paideia;* the concluding depiction of Francis, so un-Homeric and un-Pindaric, yet with his own *areté* and his Vergilian vision of the Elysian Fields (*Aeneid* 6.638–47)—these principal elements of Wilbur's poem both are based on the complex of the classical tradition and at the same time adumbrate and crystallize European culture.

There are indeed classical influences in modern poetry, more than classical mythology, even in the poetry of America written after the heyday of T. S. Eliot's dominating influence. Of course the classical elements are not nearly so ubiquitous as they used to be in English and American poetry. But for the poets who began to produce their work in the last thirty years there are so many newer influences. For older writers whose production continued into the past thirty years, like Conrad Aiken, the traditional allusions are still the best ones, as is richly illustrated by Aiken's 1958 poem "The Crystal"—based on Pythagoras, his father Mnesarchos the gem-carver, and that art—and his glittering poem on Helen, called "Portrait."[24] But these poems reflect the classical tradition that Eliot and his contemporaries knew, and theirs was a different world from that of the writers born since 1920. In the minds of the poets of today there are points of reference in addition to and on a par with those known to the earlier writers of this century. To the more recent writer, Thomas Mann and Robbe-Grillet are capable of being as meaningful and stimulating as Vergil and Sophocles. The artists of our day have behind them the experiences of two world wars and around them an atmosphere of continual international tension. Today there is such an accumulation of art, knowledge, and circumstance to influence and inform the modern artist. On the other hand, although recent poetry is not peopled regularly with sphinxes, Philomela, and the Elgin Marbles, when these poets do employ classical references they do so with force and a fresh insight. We can rejoice that alongside more recent voices and influences the classical muses continue to sing with clarity and strength.

CHAPTER SIX

Marguerite Yourcenar:
The Classicism of *Feux*
and *Mémoires d'Hadrien*

Marguerite Yourcenar's celebrated fictional auto-
biography, *Mémoires d'Hadrien*, was preceded by
a work combining surrealist technique and classical themes. This earlier work was the collection of short
stories, *Feux*.[1] Although it was largely the *Hadrien* which
brought Yourcenar's attention to the Académie Française
and gained her election to that august body in 1981,[2] in fact
Feux (1936) can be seen as a prelude to *Mémoires d'Hadrien*
(1951). It is the purpose of this study to show both works as
significant contributions to the present-day vitality of the
classical tradition.

In the preface to *Feux*, Yourcenar describes her book
"comme une série de proses lyriques reliées entre elles par
une certaine notion de l'amour" (9); "like a series of lyrical
prose pieces connected by a notion of love" (Katz ix). This is
accurate enough, but let me further describe *Feux* as a group
of cameo portraits of figures from the world of ancient
Greece and the Greek East, mainly set in the background of
Europe in the 1930s. The characters portrayed are Phaedra,
Achilles, Patroclus, Antigone, Mary Magdalene, Phaedo,
Clytemnestra, and Sappho. In addition, there is one much
less well known character, a girl named Lena, who is caught
up in the famous conspiracy of Harmodius and Aristogiton.

Thus there are nine "lyrical prose pieces," the most elaborate being the "Léna" at the center of the collection. Although Yourcenar does not account for her sources, we can see that they range from Homer to Sophocles to Athenaeus, the encyclopedist of the third century A.D. and a source of "Léna." As far as the plots of the vignettes are concerned, Yourcenar gives us very free adaptations.

In the preface Yourcenar states that "à des degrés divers, tous ces récits modernisent le passé" (11); "in various degrees, all these stories modernize the past" (Katz x). We need to observe, however, that for this work "modern" is especially the 1930s, a period when, as Yourcenar explains, there was "la passion du spectacle sous le triple aspect du ballet, du music-hall et du film, commune à toute la génération qui vers 1935 avait environ trente ans" (16); "the love of spectacles shared by the generation that in 1935 was about thirty years old [taking] the triple aspects of ballet, music hall, and film" (Katz xiv).

In its nature, Feux is very akin to contemporary works that dealt with classical antiquity from a modern point of view, such as Jean Cocteau's La Machine infernale (1934) and Jean Giraudoux's La Guerre de Troie n'aura pas lieu (1935). The surrealist painter Salvador Dali was flourishing at this time, as was the great film maker, Charles Chaplin. Nineteen thirty-five also saw the invasion of Ethiopia by Italy under the leadership of Mussolini. War was in the air, and that atmosphere is especially reflected in Yourcenar's treatment of the tyranny at Athens under the dictators, the Peisistratids, and the conspiracy against them of Harmodius and Aristogiton.

In Feux is the broad understanding of life and human nature that is so profoundly displayed in the later Hadrien. In the preface of Feux, written in 1967 after the publication of

Hadrien, Yourcenar sagely observes: "Certains passages de *Feux* me semblent aujourd'hui contenir des vérités entre-vues de bonne heure, mais qu'ensuite toute la vie n'aura pas été de trop pour essayer de retrouver et d'authentifier" (27); "Certain passages in *Fires* seem to me to contain truths glimpsed early on that needed a whole lifetime to be re-discovered and authenticated" (Katz xxii). Those truths of a lifetime are in *Hadrien,* published nearly twenty years after *Feux.*

Yourcenar's "Phèdre," the opening piece of *Feux,* evokes the mind of Euripides' tragic queen as she decides to impli-cate her stepson, Hippolytus, in her suicide. As Yourcenar states, "Elle reconstruit au fond de soi-même un Labyrinthe où elle ne peut que se retrouver" (34); "She re-creates inside herself a deep Labyrinth where she is bound to dwell again" (Katz 7).

Phaedra's contemplation of her passion for Hippolytus takes on the attributes of a surrealist poem or painting as she draws closer to her death: "Poussée par la cohue de ses an-cêtres, elle glisse le long de ces corridors de métro, pleins d'une odeur de bête, où les rames fendent l'eau grasse du Styx, où les rails luisants ne proposent que le suicide ou le départ" (36); "Pushed by the throng of her ancestors, she slides along these subway corridors filled with animal smells; here oars split the oily waters of the Styx, here shiny rails suggest either suicide or departure" (Katz 8). Yourcenar inge-niously compares the labyrinthine Palace of Minos, where Phaedra, Ariadne's sister, grew up, to a modern subway. The piece ends with Yourcenar's frustrated Phaedra grateful for the death to come.

In "Achille," we find ourselves on the island of Scyros. Your-cenar says of Achilles' mother, Thetis, "Dès que Thétis avait vu

se former dans les yeux de Jupiter le film des combats où suc-
comberait Achille, elle avait cherché dans toutes les mers du
monde une île, un roc, un lit assez étanche pour flotter sur
l'avenir" (42); "As soon as Thetis saw the film of battles Achilles
would die in, a vision being formed in Jupiter's eyes, she
sought in all the seas of the world an island, a rock, a bed so
water-tight that it could float toward the future" (Katz 13). In this
setting suggesting the work of the painter René Magritte—indeed, Yourcenar's floating-rock imagery anticipates Magritte's
Chateau des Pyrénées (1959)—Achilles is hidden by his
mother, dressed as a woman among women, but still a man
to two of the princesses there, Deidamia of mythology and
Misandra of Yourcenar's imagination.

Yourcenar has the Greek contingent arrive in search of
Achilles, the principals in the delegation being Ulysses, Patroclus, and Thersites. Achilles does *not* reveal himself in the
handling of the weapons, as is the case in the more familiar
version of the tale, so shocked is he to see that Deidamia has
suddenly fallen in love with Patroclus. The Greeks leave,
Achilles strangles Deidamia; then he runs to the beach and
leaps into the boat just being launched, like the Victory he
will be for the Greek cause.

Yourcenar's "Patrocle" is a brief study of the grieving Achilles
after the death of his friend. The war has now dragged on,
seemingly beyond measure. Yourcenar eloquently summarizes
the state of affairs: "La première génération de héros qui avaient
reçu la guerre comme un privilège, presque comme une investiture . . . fit place à un contingent de soldats qui l'acceptèrent
comme un devoir, puis la subirent comme un sacrifice" (62);
"The first generation of heroes had accepted war as a privilege,
almost an investiture; they were followed, in turn, by a contingent of soldiers who accepted it as a duty and later bore it as a
sacrifice" (Katz 27).

In this phase of sacrifice, the Amazons come into the fray and Achilles is matched in battle with Penthesilea, who wears armor of pure gold. Achilles slays the Amazon queen. The story ends as follows: "Des infirmiers s'élancaient; on entendit crépiter la mitrailleuse des prises de vue; des mains impatientes écorchaient ce cadavre d'or" (69); "Orderlies rushed forward; the sputtering of flashbulbs going off sounded like machine-gun fire; impatient hands were skinning the golden corpse" (Katz 32). When in the glare of the flashbulbs the visor is lifted, Achilles bursts into tears and "soutenait la tête de cette victime digne d'être un ami. C'était le seul être au monde qui ressemblait à Patrocle" (69); "hold[s] up the head of this victim worthy of being a friend. She was the only creature in the world who looked like Patroclus" (Katz 32).

Yourcenar's "Antigone" anticipates the tone of Jean Anouilh's modern-dress *Antigone* of 1946. Both have the setting of modern war. Yourcenar's Antigone carries the body of her dead brother, moving forward "dans cette nuit fusillée par les phares" (82); "into this night shot through by searchlights" (Katz 41).

Soon Antigone is captured and imprisoned. Creon's son, Haemon, decides to end his life with hers. The final scene is horrible, Haemon and Antigone bound together, like a pendulum, yet with, again, a surrealist beauty: "Liés l'un à l'autre comme pour peser plus lourd, leur lent va-et-vient les enfonce chaque fois plus avant dans la tombe, et ce poids palpitant remet en mouvement la machinerie des astres" (84–85); "They are tied one to the other as if to make a heavier weight; their slow oscillation drives them each time further into the grave, and this throbbing weight rewinds the machinery of the stars" (Katz 43).

It is with the centerpiece of *Feux*, "Léna," that we find ourselves confronted with a literary problem. How many readers today would appreciate a re-creating of the story of Harmodius and Aristogiton? In Yourcenar's book it is her most compelling reconstruction, a demonstration of her scholarly knowledge of ancient history. Nevertheless, the tyrannical reign of the Peisistratids in late sixth-century Athens is not an event of common knowledge, although the tale of Harmodius and Aristogiton is a set-piece for Thucydides (*Peloponnesian War* 6.54–59).

Yourcenar's Aristogiton is a boxer who lives with his servant-mistress, Lena. They go to Olympia for the games, where Aristogiton is a winner and becomes famous. Drunk with glory, Aristogiton returns to Athens not with Lena but with Harmodius, the rich friend of the dictators. Peisistratus is dead and Athens is ruled jointly now by his sons, Hippias and Hipparchus. The codictator, Hipparchus, is in love with Harmodius and thus is angry when he finds that Harmodius is now friendly to the great boxer Aristogiton.

Soon thereafter, Hipparchus visits Lena secretly for information. Shortly after this, Aristogiton is attacked by a gang of thugs. Together Lena and Harmodius begin the nursing of Aristogiton. On the evening of the Panathenaea, a bomb is thrown at Hippias and Hipparchus near the Parthenon. Harmodius and Aristogiton are caught as conspirators; Harmodius is immediately lynched by the maddened crowd. Aristogiton is sent away for execution. The innocent Lena is taken before the dying Hipparchus for interrogation by torture.

Yourcenar's "Léna" is a grim but fast-moving tale. Of course the atmosphere is that of Nazi Germany in the 1930s. As a tale of love and betrayal on several levels, it is the most absorbing piece in the book.

We see, now, Yourcenar's method in *Feux*. She takes figures out of Greek mythology or history, puts them and their generally familiar situations into a twentieth-century setting or atmosphere, essentially the 1930s, and then gives them thoughts and reactions in the manner of a surrealist stream of consciousness. Her concern is with innermost thoughts and dreams. Her characterizations are, however, uncannily "right," as far as classical myth and history are concerned, and this verisimilitude proves how significant Phaedra, Achilles, and Antigone continue to be. They speak to us as themselves in our general time, as themselves in antiquity, and as figures in the surrealist ambience.

Following "Léna," Yourcenar then has three pieces dealing with Mary Magdalene, Phaedo, and Clytemnestra. We might wonder at the inclusion of Mary Magdalene, but for Yourcenar the ancient Greek East is one world. To Yourcenar, Mary Magdalene is a figure of the Hellenistic age, as it extends into the early Roman Empire, not just to the New Testament.

In "Marie-Madeleine," the setting is any modern city of the Levant, Damascus or Beirut; Jesus and the Apostles are a subversive sect which must be dealt with by the authorities. For Mary the eventually empty tomb is a mystical experience that forces her to articulate to herself the meaning of love, especially the love of God.

Phaedo in Yourcenar's hands is a slave bought by Alcibiades and given to Socrates on the eve of the Sicilian Expedition. In this tale alone in the collection is there no suggestion of the 1930s. Yourcenar's "Phédon" focuses on the historical execution of Socrates, an event that moves the young Phaedo deeply, and an event that Yourcenar describes with accuracy, passion, and grace.

"Clytemnestre" has the consort of Agamemnon defending

herself before a jury. In the speech, the horror and ugliness of the Trojan War are stressed, making the "Clytemnestre" a companion to the earlier vignettes on Patroclus and Antigone. We are back in modern times in the "Clytemnestre." The queen greets the returning Agamemnon at the Lion Gate of Mycenae, shielding herself from the sun with a pink parasol (183). Cassandra is a Turkish fortune teller, and after dinner that evening she reads the palms of the members of the dinner party. The murders occur soon thereafter. Clytemnestra ends her address with a description of how haunted she is by her husband. Yourcenar enlarges on what Aeschylus suggests in the *Choephori*.

Yourcenar concludes her collection with "Sappho," a story based on the late Hellenistic or Roman account of the poet's love for Phaon.[3] In this lyric piece Yourcenar gives us a surrealist fantasy. Her Sappho is a trapeze artist in a traveling circus. The only happiness in her life is seeing the posters that advertise her famous aerial act. She loves one after another her companions—Gyrinno, Anactoria—but above all the girl she found as a stranger in the city, the little waif Attys. Alas for Sappho, Attys leaves her for Philippe, a tobacco importer.

Time passes, Sappho always looking in her travels for a glimpse of Attys. In Istanbul, Sappho meets Phaon and finds herself with unexpected sensations in the presence of this man. Her feelings deepen when Phaon takes her sailing on the Bosphorus. One evening, in Sappho's apartment, Phaon puts on a dressing gown that had belonged to Attys (211–12). As Penthesilea had deeply reminded Achilles of Patroclus, so too is Sappho overwhelmed by the memory of Attys. Sappho determines to use the trapeze as the instrument of her own death. In imagery that brings us back to the legend of Sappho's death by drowning, Yourcenar says of the fall into the net: "Les mailles ploient sans céder sous le poids de cette statue repêchée des profondeurs du ciel. Et bientôt les manoeuvres n'auront plus qu'à haler sur le sable ce corps de marbre pâle, ruisselant de sueur comme une noyée d'eau de mer" (216); "The meshes give but do not yield under the weight of this statue fished out from the bottom of the sky. And soon roustabouts will only have to haul onto the sand this marble pale body streaming with sweat like a drowning woman pulled from the sea"(Katz 129). The complex imagery is reminiscent of the painter Giorgio de Chirico in his surrealist period, or of the poet André Breton.

Thus ends *Feux*, Marguerite Yourcenar's set of "lyrical prose pieces" from the 1930s. Poignant and violent, comic and tragic, these passionate love stories accord well with the era of Marlene Dietrich's film *Blue Angel*, the Chaplin films, the continuing experiments of the surrealists, and the darkening of Europe as the tyrannies of Germany and Italy went rampant. *Feux* is a book of its time. It speaks to us today, as well. It is a glittering demonstration of the ever-continuous vitality of the classical tradition. Rather like Vergil, however, Yourcenar was now ready for work of greater magnitude, and of even greater meaning.

Yourcenar's *Hadrien* is a historical reconstruction first begun in 1924, but pursued seriously beginning in 1937, just after the publication of *Feux*. World War II interrupted the project, to be resumed in 1948. Yourcenar's notes on the composition of the book conclude both the French and English editions of *Hadrien*, as well as an extremely detailed bibliographical note on the ancient sources for and modern studies of Hadrian. As Moses Hadas observed in a review of the 1954 translation,[4] we are given an uncommonly intimate view of this author's "workshop." Clearly Yourcenar approached her subject with both artistic passion and scholarly zeal.

The novel is divided into six sections, each with a sonorous Latin title: "Animula Vagula Blandula"; "Varius Multiplex Multiformis"; "Tellus Stabilita"; "Saeculum Aureum"; "Disciplina Augusta"; "Patientia." The first heading is the opening line of Hadrian's famous poem, quoted in the biography attributed to Aelius Spartianus:

Animula vagula blandula
hospes comesque corporis,
quae nunc abibis in loca
pallidula rigida nudula?
nec ut soles dabis iocos!
(Scriptores Historiae Augustae,
Vita Hadriani 25.9)

Sweet, departing little soul, guest-friend, comrade of my shell, now into what dreary, dull, graceless haunts will you go? None of your old fun there!

(My translation)

The second heading, "Varius Multiplex Multiformis," comes from the Epitome Caesarum (14.6), a late imperial biographical dictionary. The other four headings, as Yourcenar explains in the notes,[5] are legends on coins of the reign.

The opening section of the novel is a prelude, a meditation addressed to Marcus Aurelius, on the brevity of life and the inevitability of death. Marcus had been a favorite member of Hadrian's court since he was a boy. Now, on his deathbed, Hadrian knows that, in time, Marcus will reign. The second part, "Varius Multiplex Multiformis," deals with the reign of Trajan, A.D. 98–117. During this period of his life Hadrian,

Trajan's ward, achieved renown as a general, especially in Upper Germany and Dacia; was named archon of Athens in 111–112; and developed his deep friendship with Trajan's consort, Plotina. It would have been during this sojourn in Athens that Hadrian began to have a passion for Greece. He went on from there to serve as governor of Syria during Trajan's war with Parthia. Upon Trajan's death in August 117, Hadrian was revealed as the heir to the throne. In "Tellus Stabilita" we have the beginning of the Hadrianic Pax Romana. Hadrian himself declares, as he contemplates world empire, "Je m'instrumentais vers de plus calmes fins. Je commençais à rêver d'une souverainetè olympienne" (115); "I was directing myself toward calmer ends. I began to dream of truly Olympian rule" (Frick 109).

Hadrian's *saeculum aureum* in Yourcenar's treatment are the years with the adored Antinous. The emperor had encountered this young man in Bithynia during the imperial tour in 124. The youth was invited to join the emperor's entourage and soon the middle-aged, childless Hadrian found himself bestowing the attention of a father, if not, indeed, the attention of a lover, upon Antinous. In A.D. 130, during a journey up the Nile, Antinous was drowned. While Antinous lived, Hadrian was happy and in his most creative years. Yourcenar calls the *saeculum aureum* "années fabuleuses" (162), "fabulous years" (Frick 154). It was the era of the completion of the Pantheon in Rome (A.D. 120) and the long-hoped-for Olympieum in Athens (A.D. 132).

"Disciplina Augusta" is the chronicle of the Jewish wars, the search for an heir, and the beginning of Hadrian's fatal illness. The Jewish wars were the darkest and most vexing period in the reign of Hadrian. Jerusalem had been destroyed by Titus in the rebellion of A.D. 70. Hadrian wanted

to rebuild the city as Aelia Capitolina; the ancient temple of
Jehovah would be replaced by one to Jupiter Capitolinus.
The rule of Rome in Palestine was an undeniable fact. The
Jewish leader, Bar Kochba, Son of the Star, however, was determined that Hadrian should not succeed, and so the new
rebellion began. Hadrian himself had to take command. Although for Hadrian the war was defensive, it was calamitous
for both armies. With his victory, the emperor was left with a
profound *Weltschmerz*. In 135, with only three years to live,
Hadrian was weary of the world. The novel ends with the
section entitled "Patientia," and by now the emperor was
dying. "A Tibur," says Yourcenar's Hadrian, visiting once
again his great estate outside of Rome, "du sein d'un mois
de mai brûlant, j'écoute sur les plages de l'île d'Achille la
longue plainte des vagues" (289); "Here in Tibur, in the full
heat of May, I listen for the waves' slow complaint on the
beach of the isle of Achilles" (Frick 278). Thinking of the
home of Achilles, Hadrian sends for Titus Aurelius An-
toninus, his heir.

Yourcenar's novel, solidly founded on the sources, and on
the research available forty years ago, is a work of the imagination. At the same time, Yourcenar's portrait is not at vari-
ance with the facts in Herbert Benario's carefully docu-
mented commentary on the *Vita Hadriani* of the *Historia
Augusta*. What would Yourcenar have done with Hadrian had
she had the wealth of information in the Benario work to use?
My guess is that the detail in the latter might have made
Yourcenar's novel a two-volume work, of a magnitude equal
to Tolstoy or Proust. As it is, working earlier and indepen-
dently of professional scholars over a period of nearly twenty
years, Yourcenar gains Benario's praise for being "remarkably
successful in evoking the character of the man."[6] After study-

ing the rich and impeccable Benario commentary on the *Vita Hadriani,* the critic can only admire all the more Yourcenar's achievement in historical reconstruction.

As a work of art *Hadrien* is equally impressive, and is one of the *maiora opera* of the twentieth century. The novel reflects an awareness of the cosmos in its immensity and the sensitivity for human beings in their isolation that frequently characterize the modern masterpiece. Yourcenar's *Hadrien* clearly ranks with such landmarks in our literary landscape as T. S. Eliot's *Four Quartets,* Conrad Aiken's play *Mr. Arcularis,* Hermann Broch's novel *The Death of Vergil,* Rainer Maria Rilke's *Duino Elegies.* The last named offers the adjective that best suits Yourcenar's *Hadrien,* "elegiac." The book is the elegiac memoir and meditation of a speaker contemplating himself in his universe. The posture is especially common to the writing of this era, going from Baudelaire to Sartre, to name two of Yourcenar's fellow countrymen, with Auden, Eliot, and Robert Lowell all participating in or sharing the same outlook. It is this philosophical approach to her subject that removes Yourcenar's work from the genre commonly known as the historical novel. I have high regard for such reconstructions as Henrik Sienkiewicz's *Quo Vadis* (1896), that vast canvas from the reign of Nero; Robert Graves's *I, Claudius* (1934), so brilliantly brought to television in recent years; Mary Renault's trilogy on Alexander, *Fire from Heaven* (1969), *The Persian Boy* (1972), and *Funeral Games* (1981). All three of these writers handle their historical subjects with consummate craftsmanship. The settings, in particular, are re-created in meticulous detail. It is noteworthy that Marguerite Yourcenar, in contrast, does not offer a description of Hadrian's architectural fantasy, the Villa at Tivoli. And here is the difference between the Yourcenar of the *Hadrien* and the ‑

average historical novelist: Yourcenar is concerned with the heart, the mind, of a human being who occupied the highest and the loneliest position in the world. In the *Hadrien* we are greatly beyond the character sketches of *Feux*. By concentrating on the mind of this person, the outward trappings of his existence scarcely noticed, Yourcenar makes the Roman emperor an Everyman. The voice in *Hadrien* has the same significance for the contemplative modern reader as the speaker in Eliot's *Little Gidding* or the protagonist of Mann's *Death in Venice*. Hadrian is all of us, we all are Hadrian.

The imagery that heightens the Yourcenar novel, making it artistically equal to contemporary achievements and much more than a latter-day *Quo Vadis* or *I, Claudius,* are the images essential to the novel of the sea and the cosmos. In the prelude Hadrian says to young Marcus, referring to the Greek islands, "Comme le voyageur qui navigue entre les îles de l'Archipel voit la buée lumineuse se lever vers le soir, et découvre peu à peu la ligne du rivage, je commence á apercevoir le profil de ma mort" (5); "Like a traveler sailing the Archipelago who sees the luminous mists lift toward evening, and little by little makes out the shore, I begin to discern the profile of my death" (Frick 5). Midway in this book, in the section entitled "Saeculum Aureum," Hadrian says of his empire, a great thalassocracy, "Je l'avais gréé comme un beau navire appareillé pour un voyage qui durera des siècles" (173); "I had rigged it like a fair ship made ready for a voyage which might last for centuries" (Frick 165). And then in Rome, after the dedication of the Pantheon, Hadrian observes that the Palatine Palace, like a marine pavilion, "[oscillait] comme les flancs d'une barque; les tentures écartées pour laisser entrer la nuit romaine étaient celles d'un pavillon de poupe; les cris de la foule étaient le bruit du vent dans les cordages" (179); "seemed to sway like a ship at sea: the curtains drawn back to admit the night air were like those of a high cabin aft, and the cries of the crowd were the sound of wind in the sails" (Frick 171). Soon thereafter, Hadrian is in Athens for the dedication of the Olympieum, and he reports, "la Grèce repartait comme un navire longtemps immobilisé par un calme, qui sent de nouveau dans ses voiles la poussée du vent" (184); "Greece was stirring again like a vessel, long becalmed, caught anew in the current of the wind" (Frick 176).

The Olympieum, dedicated to Zeus Olympius, had been begun by the dictator Peisistratus in the sixth century B.C. Long in building, the temple was part of Hadrian's plan to rejuvenate his beloved Athens. Greece had been long becalmed. The new wind was Hadrian himself. Hadrian is beside the sea at the time of his death in the imperial villa at Baiae, on the Bay of Naples, and he writes: "La vague fait sur le rivage son murmure de soie froissée et de caresse" (307); "On the shore the waves make their murmur of rustling silk and whispered caress" (Frick 295). Just before this, as quoted earlier, Hadrian had been at the Villa in Tibur listening "sur les plages de l'île d'Achille [à] la longue plainte des vagues" (289); "for the waves' slow complaint on the beach of the isle of Achilles" (Frick 278).

Of course this imagery of the sea and sailing suits well Yourcenar's much-traveled hero. Benario has an appendix devoted to the chronology of Hadrian's journeys—his imperial tours of inspection and occasional holidays—bringing up-to-date the lists of earlier scholars. Hadrian was out of Italy for parts if not all of eleven years of the twenty-two of his reign.[7]

Hadrian was one of the great travelers of all time and knew the Mediterranean well. The great crisis of his life, the death of Antinous, was a death by water. Yourcenar, also a world-class traveler, knew the oceanic voyage, as well as the sounding sea at her home on the coast of Maine.

In addition to the marine imagery, Yourcenar's *Hadrien* is suffused with a sense of cosmic grandeur, a comprehension of the infinite. It is this quality of sensitivity for man in the cosmos that gives the novel its epic tone and gives the novel a relationship not only to the world of Greece and Rome but also to the arts and the temper of the present time.

Janet Whatley compares the *Hadrien* to Walter Pater's nineteenth-century re-creation of the age of Marcus Aurelius, *Marius the Epicurean,* remarking on the effort in both works "to evoke the *whole* of classical culture, to assess its entire achievement."[8] Whatley is right and was anticipated in her appreciation by Stewart Perowne in his 1960 biography of the emperor.[9] Both Hadrian's reign and Yourcenar's evocation of it embrace the universe as it was then known. Yourcenar has Hadrian endowed with a cosmic consciousness.

At the opening of "Tellus Stabilita," Hadrian says: "La circulation de l'or, le passage des idées, aussi subtil que celui de l'air vital dans les artères recommençaient au dedans du grand corps du monde; le pouls de la terre se remettait à battre" (102); "The circulation of gold and the passage of ideas (as subtle as that of vital air in the arteries) were beginning again within the world's great body; earth's pulse began to beat once more" (Frick 96). Later, the emperor observes (as quoted above), "Je m'instrumentais vers de plus calmes fins. Je commencais à rêver d'une souveraineté olympienne" (115); "I was directing myself toward calmer ends. I began to dream of truly Olympian rule" (Frick 109).

And then Hadrian has his experience of initiation into the Eleusinian Mysteries, an experience that stays with him while he goes on to Syria, where he has a profoundly moving night of stargazing. The emperor concludes: "Mais la nuit syrienne représente ma part consciente d'immortalité" (157); "But the Syrian night remains as my conscious experience of immortality" (Frick 149).

The sense of the infinite in literature is as old as the *Iliad* (the scene, for example, of the troops beside the watchfires in 8.553–65), coming to a crescendo in Greek literature in the opening scenes of *Agamemnon*, where the sentinel waits for the signal beacon marking the end of the Trojan War. Vergil heightens the theme in the first book of the *Aeneid*, the storm at sea (1.84–156) and Jupiter's mighty prophecy (1.257–96), with another crescendo coming in the visionary conclusion of book 6 (756–892), the Rome of the future. Meanwhile, in the course of Greek and Roman literature there is frequently the demonstration of a cosmic sense or vision in the works of Sappho, the famous ode to Aphrodite; certainly Plato, the Vision of Er at the end of book 10 of the *Republic*; and I would not want to omit Lucretius, especially the preludes to books 1 and 2.

But perhaps I am belaboring a commonplace. If I am, it is because I want my estimation of the Yourcenar novel to be perfectly clear. The fact is that most high artists of any art have a sense for the infinite. Examples range from the ceiling of the Sistine Chapel by Michelangelo to the world-vision of Hans Castorp from the mountaintop in Thomas Mann's *The Magic Mountain* (1924). In more recent modern art we have Conrad Aiken's play of 1957, *Mr. Arcularis*, the tale of a sea voyage for recuperation, which ends with a thrilling description of a man's entering into the infinity of death, there ringing in his ears a paean to light. Yourcenar's Hadrian, Aiken's Mr. Arcularis, and, I would add, Hermann Broch's Vergil dying at Brundisium, have much in common as they finally attain an illuminated comprehension of universe and cosmos. Yourcenar's Hadrian near the end of his life observes:

Nos livres ne périront pas tous; on réparera nos statues brisées; d'autres coupoles et d'autres frontons naîtront de nos frontons et de nos coupoles; quelques hommes penseront, travailleront et sentiront comme nous; j'ose compter sur ces continuateurs placés à intervalles irréguliers le long des siècles, sur cette intermittente immortalité. (306)

Not all our books will perish, nor our statues, if broken, lie unrepaired; other domes and other pediments will arise from our domes and pediments; some few men will think and work and feel as we have done, and I venture to count upon such continuators, placed irregularly throughout the centuries, and upon this kind of intermittent immortality. (Frick 293)

Following this clear view into the future, at death Hadrian addresses his soul: "Un instant encore, regardons ensemble les rives familières, les objets que sans doute nous ne reverrons plus. . . . Tâchons d'entrer dans la mort les yeux ouverts" (308); "But one moment still, let us gaze together on these familiar shores, on these objects which doubtless we shall not see again. . . . Let us try, if we can, to enter into death with open eyes" (Frick 295).

If Yourcenar's novel has not been so well appreciated in our country as it might be, it is, perhaps, because it deals with a nearly absolute monarch ruling at the apogee of his empire. Such a ruler and such a state are uncongenial to our egalitarian times. Yourcenar's deep research makes for a problem as well. There are so many names and circumstances from an antique era to be managed by the modern reader with little

Greek, Latin, or ancient history background. We saw a similar problem in *Feux*. The same problem could be assigned to Tolstoy's *War and Peace*. Once, however, the reader is only a few pages into the novel, the sheer humanity of *Hadrien* becomes enthralling.[10]

We have in Yourcenar's *Hadrien* a modern masterpiece. Yourcenar's Hadrian is a creation of wonderful imagination, as well as a creation of exemplary study and research. Emperor or no, Yourcenar's Hadrian poignantly illustrates Vergil's profound observation, *Sunt lacrimae rerum, et mentem mortalia tangunt* (*Aeneid* 1.462). The novel illumines the human condition in all its complexity, ambiguity, and yearning for meaning, as do the well-known masterworks of the twentieth century. And Yourcenar's Hadrian as a character is not an unfit companion for Vergil's Aeneas and Homer's Achilles. I believe that Yourcenar hoped that her hero would have this stature, and thus she has Hadrian listening to the sea at the end of his life. He hears "sur les plages de l'île d'Achille la longue plainte des vagues" (289); "the waves' slow complaint on the beach of the isle of Achilles" (Frick 278)—a tidal echo of the earlier work, *Feux*.[11]

Marguerite Yourcenar—how well she deserved her election among the Immortals of the French Academy. In grandeur of conception and beauty of execution, *Mémoires d'Hadrien* is a book for the ages.[12]

Epilogue:
Toward the End
of the Century

The *Argo* of our time has taken the form of the spaceship. The craft that took the American astronauts to the moon in 1969 was called Apollo-Saturn. As with the ancients invoking god by many names, so the double name of the spaceship seemed to ask for all good luck from every quarter.

The spaceship is symbolic of the nature of our life in the latter part of the twentieth century, and as a military machine it is a symbol for the whole century. Ours has been an era of almost constant war, with its accompanying daily anxiety and fear. There is no one alive whose life has not been affected by the world wars of this century and the chronic tensions in Central America, central Europe and the Far East.

It is little wonder that we find ourselves identifying so well with the Age of Pericles and the ensuing years of the Peloponnesian War. We do not find the Athenian domination of the Aegean basin odious, because it was done in the name of self-defense against the behemoth of the Persian Empire. The Communist presence in Cuba and Central America has been as worrisome to Americans as the Persian presence to the Greeks, until the time of Alexander the Great. We condone the conquests of Alexander because they meant the liberation of the Ionian Greeks and the removal of an enemy that had been a source of dread to Greece for nearly three hundred years.

The admiration that Alexander has generally enjoyed, and Pericles before him, shows that although people loathe a tyrant, they readily follow a strong leader. Franklin Roosevelt was extraordinarily powerful and charismatic, as was Woodrow Wilson before him. (Adolph Hitler had to be unmasked before he was known to his own people for what he was.) The two American leaders have presented themselves as forces for good and as loving guides and protectors of their people. Thus it has been natural for many people of the West, and certainly in America, during the twentieth century to be fascinated by the character of King Oedipus, a father to his people, and the story of the royal house of Thebes.

Oedipus and his daughter, Antigone, are captivating characters, whether in presentations of the original *Oedipus Rex* and *Antigone* or in such modern versions as described in the theater essay. Oedipus is a mirror both for impulsive youth and for those in middle age who have begun to see what their destiny is and know that it cannot be changed. Antigone is a champion of both freedom and principle. Antigone is also a woman standing tall in a man's world. As a character she is emblematic of the feminist movement, one of the great adjustments in the society of the twentieth century.

In their nonconformity—Oedipus in his rejection of Teiresias and established religion, Antigone's opposition to established authority—Oedipus and Antigone have qualities of Homer's Achilles. Oedipus, Antigone, Achilles—all three are Outsiders. A unifying theme in the foregoing essays, as emphasized in the discussion of Broch's Vergil, has been the motif of the Outsider, a figure very prominent in our time from Rilke to Pollock.[1] Mann's Gustav exists alone and admires from afar. Pablo Picasso in his sheer superiority exists alone; as determined, conquering artist, Picasso has all of the *areté* of Achilles. Broch's Vergil agonizes over his life, his art, the meaning of both, as much as Achilles does in book 9 of the *Iliad* just before the embassy visits him in his tent. The French playwrights of the 1920s and 1930s were drawn to the Oedipus figure, as we have seen. Giraudoux gives the problem a twist by making Hector the lonely man with impossible decisions. Eliot's Harry, searching for himself, can be seen as a fusion of Oedipus and Achilles. All three of the American poets are fundamentally concerned with a search for self and the meaning of life. Finally, there is the most powerful, most richly endowed of searchers, Yourcenar's Hadrian. He possesses the world; he searches over it. The spirit of Achilles haunts Yourcenar's Hadrian, and he reflects upon Achilles at the end of his life. I feel, as I observe in my essay, that Hadrian saw himself as a latter-day Achilles, and Yourcenar wants her hero to have the austere nobility of Homeric Achilles.

In their uses of and admiration for classical antiquity, Eliot and Picasso offer us especially cogent examples of the continuous vitality of classical themes and concepts. Picasso transforms the lyre-playing Achilles' tent into the sculptor's studio. The artist does not brood, but he does create images so advanced that much of the world will not understand them. The sculptor has deeply informed principles and is a master of his craft. He is oblivious of the world. His simultaneous admiration of the ancient world and the modern Cubist world creates a tension in the studio and in his art. Achilles, too, reveres another world, one that seems to have passed. The values of that world come to life, however, as Achilles seeks vengeance for the death of Patroclus.

Eliot first gives us the observing, searching outsider, as

Teiresias in *The Waste Land*. Teiresias becomes translated into Harry in *The Family Reunion*, but Harry also has his Achilles side. Harry's condescending, domineering family become an Agamemnon to his Achilles. Harry can only leave Wishwood. He no more knows what his end will be than does Achilles as he sits in his tent, alone, hearing the petition of Priam at the end of the *Iliad*. Eliot later created a variant of Harry Monchensey in his Celia Coplestone of *The Cocktail Party* (1949). Celia is another solitary searcher. She finds this world too much and herself too much of this world. She can only leave it, to find herself, paying a price such as that paid by Oedipus and Antigone. The ancient world was so communal—the Olympic Games, the Panathenaia, the pageants on the Campus Martius in Imperial Rome. The literature of those people, however, emphasizes the individual, and that person is ever the Outsider.

The world of archaeological discovery, both in Greek lands and in Italy, has its reflection in modern art. Picasso grew up among plaster casts of classical Greek art and then had his meaningful trip to Italy in 1917. The Roman Italy which Picasso saw would have been little different from that which Henry James saw in 1900. Progress in excavation was slowly being made at the great sites. The Roman Forum, however, even half covered up, had always been one of the most romantic and evocative sights in the world.

It was Benito Mussolini who in the 1920s and early 1930s gave lavishly of the state's resources for the recovery of Imperial Rome. The magnificent boulevard, Via dei Fori Imperiali, which stretches from the Piazza Venezia, where the dictator had his headquarters, to the Colosseum, sets off to grandiose advantage the Forum Romanum, the Forum of Augustus, and the Forum of Trajan. This was the Rome that Her-

Pablo Picasso, *Studio with Plaster Head.* Summer 1925. Oil on canvas, 38⅝″ × 51⅝″. Collection, The Museum of Modern Art, New York. Purchase.

Pablo Picasso, *Three Women at the Spring*. Summer 1921. Oil on canvas, 6'8¼" × 68½". Collection, The Museum of Modern Art, New York. Gift of Mr. and Mrs. Allan D. Emil.

mann Broch would have known—the Rome of majestic, awe-some remnants of the heart of the empire, the scene of Augustan state pageantry, and lately the scene of Il Duce's panoply.[2] Vergil was caught up in this world. He was part and parcel of this world as he lay on the imperial yacht headed for Brundisium. Should he and his poem remain forever identified with this world, such a world? Thus Broch takes up Vergil's dilemma, and he gives a victory to both Augustus and Vergil.

With the liberation of Rome at the end of World War II, a new life sprang up in the great old city, *la dolce vita* (as adumbrated by Federico Fellini's film of the same title, 1960). Rome was thronged with tourists in the 1950s and 1960s, countless numbers from the United States. For many visitors the brilliant sidewalk life of the Via Veneto was more intriguing than the silent spectacle of the monuments of the "Via dell' Impero." Nevertheless, with Rome and Pompeii open, many scholars and serious students also hastened to Italy. The School of Classical Studies in the American Academy in Rome took on a quickened life. Near Naples the classical summer school of the Vergilian Society of America offered no fewer than five study-tours per summer around the bay and in Campania. Into this world came the three American poets of my essay. It was a world that commingled Rome in all of its artistic and historical facets, scholarship, *la dolce vita*, visits to the grand hotels in Naples bordering the Via Partenope, and strolls through Pompeii.

We see now that the classical tradition as a creative stimulus for twentieth-century artists embraces mythology, the mythology as molded by the ancient writers. The formal literature of the ancients is both stimulus and resource. The history of the Greeks and Romans awes and instructs. The presence of the classical past in its impressive monuments, as well as the setting of those monuments, excite the imagination. The classical tradition is a *carmen perpetuum,* in Ovid's phrase at the opening of the *Metamorphoses.* The choristers of this continuous song are not, in the twentieth century, the old massed choir whose steady unwavering devotional hymn is heard, for example, from the poetry of Keats and Shelley. The choristers today sing from scattered chapels with a more pronounced effect from some locations than from others. These chapels are, however, integral and defined parts of the cathedral of art. Students at every level are going to be examining the classical imagery in Mann's *Death in Venice* as long as books are being read. The reputation of Marguerite Yourcenar's *Hadrien* is going to grow into the next century, and the book will be regarded as a twentieth-century monument.

A most arresting and pointed expression of the vitality of the classical tradition amid the art and life of the twentieth century is found, I believe, in the union of Paul Manship's statue of *Prometheus* (1934) and Rockefeller Center in New York City. The gilded fire-bearer both soars and hovers above the ice-skating rink in the center of the immense complex. The speeding figure is charged with energy, a beatific smile upon his face. The figure is a human spaceship, and humanity triumphant.

Prometheus is knowledge. In his legend he is the tortured victim, the savior of humanity, the enemy of tyranny. He is the original, the archetypal Outsider. In 1934, at the depth of the Great Depression, Rockefeller Center and the statue would have represented hope to an economically beleaguered world. Fifty years later, the untarnished Prometheus represents persistent vitality, creative energy, the endurance of the good. As the statue endures, gleamingly, so does its being as a work of art endure.[3]

It is not difficult to understand Prometheus as the embodiment of both art and the artist. In his strength, determination, daring and foresight, Prometheus is the artist of every art. In the context of this book, then, the Paul Manship *Prometheus* in Rockefeller Center combines with Picasso's later minotaurs as symbols of the present-day vitality of the classical tradition. This tradition ranges from Mann and Eliot, children of the nineteenth century, who grew up immersed in the classical tradition; to Hermann Broch at mid-century, who saw the past gravely threatened by tyranny and war; to Frederick Nicklaus and Richard Wilbur, who went to Rome and reacted as pure artists to the deepest and richest city in the world. Like Prometheus, all of these artists saw and caught the spark, using its energy for the firing of their modern works. Their power and energy are that of the *Guernica Bull*. Their creations, their golden Prometheus, will live forever.

Notes

Introduction

1. During January 22–23, 1958, the American Council of Learned Societies presented a program at Indiana University, Bloomington, entitled "The Present-Day Vitality of the Classical Tradition." The program embraced theater, music, and literature. The papers presented at this meeting were later published in Whitney J. Oates, ed., *From Sophocles to Picasso: The Present-Day Vitality of the Classical Tradition* (Bloomington: Indiana University Press, 1962).

2. Cf. the present author's "Vergil's Dido in Modern Literature" (Flaubert's Emma Bovary, James's Milly Theale, Williams's Blanche DuBois), *Classical and Modern Literature* 1 (Summer 1981): 267–73.

3. Harry C. Rutledge, "Greece and Rome in the Twentieth Century: Observations on the Classical Tradition and Modernism," *Classical Journal* 78 (December–January 1982–83): 143–49.

4. Rainer Maria Rilke, *Duino Elegies,* 4th ed., trans. J. B. Leishman and Stephen Spender (London: Hogarth Press, 1963), 16–17.

5. A feature of the *originality* of the great artists of the twentieth century with whom my study is concerned is that they *chose* to use classical antiquity as both starting place and theme. Richard Shiff in his recent book on Cézanne makes this point with regard to Poussin, in Poussin's combination of originality and tradition (as noted in the nineteenth century by such critics as Paul Mantz and Eugéne Delacroix); with reference to Poussin's interest in antique statuary, "their originality had both become his own originality and enabled his originality to manifest itself." Richard Shiff, *Cézanne and the End of Impressionism: A Study of the Theory, Technique, and Critical Evaluation of Modern Art* (Chicago: University of Chicago Press, 1984), 177, 181.

1. The Olympian World of Thomas Mann

1. For this essay the German text is Thomas Mann, *Ausgewählte Erzählungen* (Stockholm: Bermann-Fischer Verlag, 1945), referred to as AE; the English translation is by H. T. Lowe-Porter, *Stories of Three Decades* (New York: Alfred A. Knopf, 1936), referred to as STD. Useful to this study have been Eva Brann, "The Venetian Phaedrus," *College* 24 (July 1972): 1–9; Roberto Fertonani, "Echi Classici in *Der Tod in Venedig* di Thomas Mann," *Annali della Facoltà di Lettere e Filosofia dell' Università degli Studi di Milano* 28 (January–August 1975): 17–26; André von Gronicka, "Myth plus Psychology: A Stylistic Analysis of *Death in Venice*," in *Thomas Mann: A Collection of Critical Essays*, ed. Henry Hatfield (Englewood Cliffs, N.J.: Prentice-Hall, 1964), 46–61; Herbert Lehnert, "Thomas Mann's Early Interest in Myth and Erwin Rohde's *Psyche*," *Publications of the Modern Language Association* 79 (June 1964): 297–304; Franz H. Mautner, "Die griechischen Anklänge in Thomas Manns *Tod in Venedig*," in *Wort und Wesen: Kleinere Schriften zur Literatur und Sprache* (Frankfurt: Insel Verlag, 1974), 178–86; Thomas Mann, *Der Tod in Venedig*, ed. T. J. Reed, Clarendon German Series (Oxford: Oxford University Press, 1971); Ernst A. Schmidt, " 'Platonismus' und 'Heidentum' in Thomas Manns *Tod in Venedig*," *Antike und Abendland* 20 (1974): 151–78. Reed and Schmidt offer complete bibliographies as of their publication dates. Also useful has been the unpublished paper of Amos Lee Laine and C. Wayne Tucker, "*Death in Venice:* Mann, Britten, and the Greeks" (presented at the annual meeting of the Classical Association of the Middle West and South, University of Iowa, April 1977). The present study is concerned only with the presence and significance of classical allusions in Mann's novella. The influence of Wagner and Nietzsche on Mann has been much discussed. The Visconti film of *Death in Venice* (1971) and the Britten-Piper opera (1973) are not concerns of this essay. The English translations of Plato are from *The Collected Di-*

alogues of Plato Including the Letters, ed. Edith Hamilton and Huntington Cairns, Bollingen Series (New York: Pantheon, 1961). The translation of *Phaedrus* is by R. Hackforth; the translation of *Symposium* is by Michael Joyce. The section references correspond both to the Bollingen edition and the Oxford Classical Text (ed. John Burnet, 1957).

2. Mautner, "Die griechischen Anklänge," 185; see Mann, *Der Tod in Venedig,* ed. Reed, 168, n. 91, for Xenophon's anecdote of Critobulos kissing Alcibiades' son (*Memorabilia* 1.3), and cf. Lorraine Gustafson, "Xenophon and *Der Tod in Venedig,*" *Germanic Review* 21 (October 1946): 209–14.

3. Von Gronicka, "Myth plus Psychology," 59–60.

4. Ibid, 60; Mautner, "Die griechischen Anklänge," 180–81. Lehnert's paper is devoted to Mann's use of Erwin Rohde's 1907 work, *Psyche: Seelencult und Unsterblichkeitsglaube der Griechen* (Tübingen: Verlag von J. C. B. Mohr [Paul Siebeck], 1925). Lehnert ("Mann's Early Interest," 299) remarks on Mann's penciled copy of Rohde. Reed (Mann, *Der Tod in Venedig,* 56) notes that Rohde's book is part of the Thomas Mann–Archiv in Zurich. Lehnert (300, n. 16) also remarks on the mythology book Mann used: Friedrich Nosselt, *Lehrbuch der griechischen und römischen Mythologie für höhere Töchterschulen und die Gebildeten des weiblichen Geschlechts* (1865). Reed (56) reports that the one primary source with Mann's annotations in the Zurich archive is Rudolf Kassner's 1903 translation in German of the *Symposium.* As Lehnert observes, "Mann was not interested in the accumulation and exposition of learned material" (304). Nevertheless, Mann's understanding of ancient culture and its literature was acutely perceptive.

5. The translations of Homer are Richmond Lattimore's: *The Iliad* (Chicago: University of Chicago Press, 1961), and *The Odyssey* (New York: Harper and Row, 1967).

6. This passage, beginning with the phrase, "The sun, they say, dazzles," is closely related to Plutarch's *Erotikos,* "The Dialogue on

Love," *Moralia,* trans. W. C. Helmbold (Cambridge, Mass.: Loeb Classical Library, 1961), 764A–765A. Reed (Mann, *Der Tod in Venedig,* 171, n. 123) alerts the reader to the source; Schmidt (" 'Platonismus' und 'Heidentum,' " 160–62) sets the Mann text against Plutarch's. As Helmbold notes, "This whole passage reshapes in a condensed and continuous form a number of separate *motifs* of the *Phaedrus:* see 241a, 253e–254a, and, in general, 250–256e" (Plutarch, *Moralia,* trans. Helmbold, 403). Schmidt's paper is a major discussion of how Mann-Aschenbach manipulate Socratic themes to their own special purposes.

7. Mann's own feelings are reflected in this passage, if not throughout the novella. Mann was always attracted to handsome young men. Cf. Richard Winston, *Thomas Mann: The Making of an Artist, 1875–1911* (New York: Alfred A. Knopf, 1981), 273–74; Thomas Mann, *Diaries 1918–1939,* trans. Richard Winston and Clara Winston (New York: Harry N. Abrams, 1982), cf. entries for 14 July 1920, 31 October 1920, 26 July 1921, 25 April 1934. The passion of the older Aschenbach for the boy, Tadzio, suits the analysis of *erastes* and *eromenos* in K. J. Dover, *Greek Homosexuality* (Cambridge, Mass.: Harvard University Press, 1978).

8. The beloved of Eos: Orion (Homer, *Odyssey* 5.121f.), Cleitos (Homer, *Odyssey* 15.250), Cephalus (Hesiod, *Theogony* 986). Lehnert ("Mann's Early Interest," 300) notes Mann's use of Rohde for the dawn scene.

9. See the tangentially interesting essay "The Breakdown of Gustav von Aschenbach" in Thorkil Vanggaard, *Phallós: A Symbol and Its History in the Male World* (New York: International Universities Press, 1972), 183–204, esp. 189.

10. See Lehnert, "Mann's Early Interest," 301, on the relevant passages in Rohde.

11. Peter Heller, *"Der Tod in Venedig* und Thomas Manns *Grund-Motiv,"* in *Thomas Mann: Ein Kolloquium,* ed. Hans H. Schulte and Gerald Chapple (Bonn: Bouvier Verlag Herbert Grundmann, 1978), 41, 60, 45.

12. Schmidt, " 'Platonismus' und 'Heidentum,' " 170, 174.

13. Lehnert, "Mann's Early Interest," 298.

2. The Resonant World of Picasso

1. William Rubin, ed., *Pablo Picasso: A Retrospective,* chronology by Jane Fluegel (New York: Museum of Modern Art, 1980), 312. The Picasso retrospective, which occupied the entire Museum of Modern Art in the spring and summer of 1980, was one of the most comprehensive exhibits of a single artist ever staged. No account of Picasso can fail to consider the Rubin catalog of the 1980 show, with its scholarly chronology. This essay is keyed by page number to the Rubin catalog.

2. Arthur Evans, *The Palace of Minos* (1921–36; reprint, New York: Biblo and Tannen, 1964), 3 : 212–13. For the international fame of the project cf. Sylvia L. Horwitz, *The Find of a Lifetime: Sir Arthur Evans and the Discovery of Knossos* (New York: Viking Press, 1981), 97, 101, 141.

3. Wilhelm Boeck and Jaime Sabartés, *Picasso* (New York: Harry N. Abrams, 1955), 193.

4. Hans Bolliger, Introduction to *Picasso's "Vollard Suite,"* trans. Norbert Guterman (New York: Harry N. Abrams, 1977), 94–97.

5. See Caroline Houser, *Dionysus and His Circle: Ancient Through Modern* (Cambridge, Mass.: Fogg Art Museum, Harvard University, 1979), 94–97. Houser with admirable economy summarizes many of Picasso's classical sources. She does not deal with *Minotauromachy* or *Guernica,* neither one being Dionysiac in inspiration. In the Houser catalog, Diane Upright Headley's appreciation of the aquatint from the *Suite Vollard* is exquisite.

6. Robert Hughes, *The Shock of the New* (New York: Alfred A. Knopf, 1981), 151: "The Vollard Suite is saturated in nostalgia, which, like every other emotion in Picasso's work, is expressed with total candour. It was in fact the last major work of art, by Picasso or anyone else, to be directly inspired by Mediterranean an-

tiquity: the end of an immense tradition that died amid the historical disjuncture, the irony, suffering, and physical ruin brought on by war and peace in the twentieth century." Hughes, in his concern for the plastic arts, omits consideration of such writers later in the century as Marguerite Yourcenar.

7. Bolliger, Introduction to Picasso's "Vollard Suite," xi. Plate numbers in the text refer to this edition.

8. William S. Lieberman, Introduction to *The Sculptor's Studio: Etchings by Picasso* (New York: Museum of Modern Art, 1952), 2.

9. Abraham Horodisch, *Picasso as a Book Artist*, trans. I. Grafe, (New York: World, 1962), 42–43. Horodisch (114–17) presents a full description of Picasso's book illustrations, with a minutely detailed bibliography divided into such categories as "Books Containing Illustrations Which Form an Evident Unity with the Text."

10. Horodisch, *Picasso as a Book Artist*, 43.

11. Ibid., 46.

12. Boeck and Sabartés, *Picasso*, 188.

13. See Harry C. Rutledge, "Classical Latin Poetry: An Art for Our Time," in *The Endless Fountain: Essays on Classical Humanism*, ed. Mark Morford (Columbus: Ohio State University Press, 1972), 138–39.

14. Maurice Raynal, *Picasso*, trans. James Emmons (Lausanne: Albert Skira, 1953), 77.

15. The following presentation is that of a classicist looking at Picasso's painting and analyzing it for its content as related to Picasso's classicism in several years immediately preceding the creation of *Guernica*. The bibliography on *Guernica* is voluminous, embracing fifty-three references in Ray Anne Kibbey, *Picasso: A Comprehensive Bibliography* (New York: Garland, 1977). Rudolf Arnheim, *Picasso's "Guernica": The Genesis of a Painting* (Berkeley and Los Angeles: University of California Press, 1962) includes all of the preliminary sketches and drawings made in preparation for the mural. See also Boeck and Sabartés, *Picasso*, 225–39; Otto J. Brendel, "Classic and Non-Classic Elements in Picasso's *Guernica*," in *From*

Sophocles to Picasso, ed. Oates, 120–59; Max Raphael, "Discord Between Form and Content: Picasso, *Guernica*" in *The Demands of Art,* trans. Norbert Guterman, Bollingen Series, no. 78 (Princeton, N.J.: Princeton University Press, 1968), 135–79. It should be noted that Max Raphael died in 1952; the papers in his book were collected posthumously. The Brendel essay was first given as a paper at a conference at Indiana University in January 1958 on "The Present-Day Vitality of the Classical Tradition," sponsored by the American Council of Learned Societies.

16. Raphael, *The Demands of Art,* 175.

17. Arnheim (Picasso's "Guernica," 27) reads left to right; Brendel ("Classic and Non-Classic Elements," 130, 142) and Raphael (*The Demands of Art,* 140, 153) read right to left.

18. Brendel, "Classic and Non-Classic Elements," 139–40, 137.

19. Raphael, *The Demands of Art,* 154–55.

20. Brendel, "Classic and Non-Classic Elements," 127.

21. Raphael, *The Demands of Art,* 145.

22. David Douglas Duncan, *Picasso's Picassos* (New York: Harper and Brothers, 1961), 155.

3. Archetypal Hellas

1. The French text used herein for both Gide's *Oedipe* and Cocteau's *La Machine infernale* is that with introduction and notes by William S. Bell (New York: Dell, 1968), hereafter cited parenthetically in the text as Bell. The English translation of *Oedipe* by John Russell in André Gide, *Two Legends: Oedipus and Theseus* (New York: Vintage Books, 1958) has been useful; this edition is hereafter cited as Russell in the text. An abbreviated version of this study was presented before the Southern Section of the Classical Association of the Middle West and South, Vanderbilt University, 2 November 1984.

2. Cf. Helen Watson-Williams, *André Gide and the Greek Myth: A Critical Study* (Oxford: Clarendon Press, 1967), 119: "It is perhaps

on account of their awareness of changing tastes and ideas that the modern authors distinguish themselves from the predecessors who similarly made use of the ancient myths. Where the earlier writers modified their given matter they did so without discussion. When the twentieth-century writer appears to be deliberately conforming to the taste of his age, he takes care also to express his personal point of view. Gide, for instance, declares that he now wishes to expose 'l'envers du décor' of Oedipus's story, even if such a view diminishes the emotional impact." Watson-Williams's reference is to Gide's *Journal* of 2 January 1933.

3. See n. 1 above for the French text. For the English translation I have used Jean Cocteau, *Orpheus, Oedipus Rex, The Infernal Machine*, trans. Carl Wildman (London: Oxford University Press, 1962), hereafter cited in the text as Wildman.

4. See the photograph of Queen Marie seated on a leopard skin and framed by lilies in Robert K. Massie and Jeffrey Finestone, *The Last Courts of Europe: A Royal Family Album, 1860–1914* (New York: Vendome Press, 1981), plate 289. Marie was queen consort, 1914–27.

5. The last act of *La Machine infernale* strikes critics variously. Neal Oxenhandler, *Scandal and Parade: The Theater of Jean Cocteau* (New Brunswick, N.J.: Rutgers University Press, 1957): "It is only in the fourth and final act that the play abruptly merges into the mythic world of Sophocles" (144); "The first three acts of the play are a kind of brilliant preparation in a minor key of comedy for Act IV in which the tragedy of Oedipus hits us with full dramatic force" (162). William S. Bell in his introduction (see n. 1 above): "The final act is an even more concentrated version of *Oedipe-Roi*. Almost immediately Oedipus learns the truth about his past, and the action moves precipitately toward its tragic conclusion. Thus the ritual has been accomplished, Oedipus has attained the classical glory he sought. He has, by blinding himself, collaborated with the Gods in producing a life and a destiny which is itself a masterpiece" ("*Oedipe*"; "*La Machine infernale*," 49). Cf. Leo Aylen, *Greek Tragedy and the Modern World* (London: Methuen,

1964), 265: "Oedipus is the type of the rational man. He would not believe in oracles. This is the sort of thing that a modern writer can do for his time. But it is something very much less than what the Greek poets did. There is strength in this play, but all the strength lies in what remains of the Sophocles version."

6. Jean Cocteau, *Orphée* (Paris: Librairie Stock, 1957), hereafter cited as Cocteau in the text. A close English translation is by John Savacool in *The Infernal Machine and Other Plays by Jean Cocteau* (New York: New Directions, 1963), hereafter cited as Savacool in the text.

7. The initial letters of the one-line poem "Madame Eurydice reviendra des enfers" form the word *merde*.

8. The recent critics make little of the classical analogies for *Orphée*. Francis Steegmuller is satisfied with Heurtebise as an angel derived from Cocteau's own poem "L'Ange Heurtebise"; the name is the French equivalent of "Windybank" or "Wuthering Heights" (*Cocteau: A Biography* [Boston: Little, Brown, 1970], 350–52). Oxenhandler merely observes, "Heurtebise, who is a guardian angel, is a Christian anachronism in this play about Greece" (*Scandal and Parade*, 99). Lydia Crowson remarks generally on the blend of Greek and Christian elements in the play: Eurydice and Orpheus can be seen as Mary and Joseph, Heurtebise an angel (*The Esthetic of Jean Cocteau* [Hanover, N.H.: University Press of New England, 1978], 29–30). Aylen (*Greek Tragedy*) makes no reference to Vergil. Steegmuller does note: "The play is now recognizable by all as a homosexual's imaginative deformation of a legend which, in its previous versions by Virgil and Ovid, Shelley and Rilke, Poliziano, Lope de Vega and Calderón, Glück, Rameau, Offenbach and many another, had already been presented in any way its author wished" (*Cocteau*, 364). There seems to be no connection between Rilke's *Sonnets to Orpheus* of 1922 and Cocteau's 1925 *Orpheus*. A generous bibliography on Orphic literature is offered by Charles Segal, "Rilke's *Sonnets to Orpheus* and the Orphic Tradition," *Literatur in Wissenschaft und Unterricht* 15 (1982): 367–80.

9. Georges Lemaitre, *Jean Giraudoux: The Writer and His Work*

(New York: Frederick Ungar, 1971), 103: "With marvelous virtuosity and ingenuity, Giraudoux hovers between the stately ideal of classical antiquity, with its regular beauty, its poetic charm, its mythical remoteness, and the reality of human experience packed with emotion, humor, and laughter." Texts: Jean Giraudoux, *Le Théatre complet de Jean Giraudoux* (Paris: Ides et Calendes, 1946), cited as Giraudoux in the text; *Tiger at the Gates (La Guerre de Troie n'aura pas lieu),* trans. Christopher Fry (New York: Oxford University Press, 1955), cited as Fry in the text.

10. The New York production of *Tiger at the Gates* in October 1955 was memorable among other things for the great beauty of Diane Cilento as Helen. I take Giraudoux's Helen as worthy of Homer and Marlowe. I cannot agree with Aylen: "The impact of the play is weakened by trivializing Helen" (*Greek Tragedy,* 273).

11. Lemaitre, *Jean Giraudoux,* 163: "Giraudoux, who was thoroughly versed in Greek culture, probably drew from the Greek tragic poets the feeling that the major tragedy in human experience is the hopeless, desperate struggle of a human against overwhelming, crushing destiny."

12. Cf. Barbara W. Tuchman, *The March of Folly: From Troy to Vietnam* (New York: Alfred A. Knopf, 1984), chap. 2, "Prototype: The Trojans Take the Wooden Horse Within Their Walls."

13. Cf. Francis Fergusson, *The Idea of a Theater* (Garden City, N.Y.: Doubleday, Anchor Books, 1949), on Cocteau's *Infernal Machine:* "The 'Thebes' which is established in the first scene by the slangy gossip of the soldiers: its cafés throbbing with popular music, hot or blue; its rising prices and its threat of revolution or war—even the menace of the 'Sphinx' which the authorities cannot deal with—might be any demoralized Balkan or Mediterranean commercial city of our time or any time" (210–11). Oxenhandler on Orphée and Eurydice: "They argue and nag each other like any young couple in boulevard comedy. They are . . . uncomplicated and eminently recognizable. They seem to be transplanted from some boulevard comedy into the world of myth with no visible

strain" (*Scandal and Parade*, 101). Lemaitre: "A work of Giraudoux hardly ever presents a continuous logical development of ideas. It is more like familiar, desultory talk. The bulk of the work consists of factual statements intermingled with allusions, remarks, and commentaries, sometimes intended to link the facts, sometimes merely suggested by association" (*Jean Giraudoux*, 189). Watson-Williams in an aside on Cocteau: "Cocteau goes on to claim that he has set both his *Oedipe* and his *Antigone* 'au rythme de notre époque'" (*Gide and the Greek Myth*, 119; the reference is to the introduction to Cocteau's *Oedipe-Roi*, [Paris: Plon, 1928], 1–2).

14. T. S. Eliot, *The Family Reunion*, in *The Complete Poems and Plays* (New York: Harcourt, Brace and World, 1952; with 1971 copyright by Esme Valerie Eliot). Page references will be designated by CPP.

15. It is not my intention to offer a new, thorough analysis of Eliot's play. My treatment is comparative. The play has been much discussed. See the bibliographies by Mildred Martin, *A Half-Century of Eliot Criticism: An Annotated Bibliography of Books and Articles in English, 1916–1965* (Lewisburg, Pa.: Bucknell University Press, 1972); and Beatrice Ricks, *T. S. Eliot: A Bibliography of Secondary Works* (Metuchen, N.J.: Scarecrow Press, 1980). The parallels between Eliot's drama and the Aeschylean original were generally outlined soon after the play's initial production by Maud Bodkin, *The Quest for Salvation in an Ancient and a Modern Play* (London: Oxford University Press, 1941).

16. Cf. Ronald Bush, *T. S. Eliot: A Study in Character and Style* (New York: Oxford University Press, 1983), 189–93 for the homecoming theme as originating in "Burnt Norton" (1935) and as developed in *The Family Reunion*.

17. Bush, remarks that Eliot's "impulse to *himself* express a 'commonplace message' in a language any educated person's mother could understand was one of the dominant aims of Eliot's late work. It supported the writing of *The Rock, Murder in the Cathedral*, and *The Family Reunion*" (*T. S. Eliot*, 161). F. O. Mat-

thiessen, however, did not care for Eliot's "effort to approximate colloquial speech"; see *The Achievement of T. S. Eliot: An Essay on the Nature of Poetry* (New York: Oxford University Press, 1959), 166.
    18. Bodkin's generalization on *The Family Reunion* suits the achievement of all four of my authors as re-creators of the antique: "In the play of Eliot the same theme of wisdom, salvation, through suffering, is wrought out in terms of present-day life and of new psychological insight. We are shown personal despair and impotence—outcome of evil relationship blindly suffered and reproduced—transformed in a moment of understanding and of personal relationship sacramentally complete" (*Quest for Salvation*, 42). Thus our Oedipus, Jocasta, Orpheus, Hector, Andromache, and Orestes.

4. Art and Power

    1. The German text on which this essay is based is Hermann Broch, *Der Tod des Vergil: Roman* (Frankfurt am Main: Suhrkamp Verlag, 1976). This edition, edited by the Broch scholar Paul M. Lutzeler, contains Broch's own commentary on the composition of his work (457–505) and the editor's history of the five versions of the novel (509–18). Essential to the present essay is the English translation by Jean Starr Untermeyer, *The Death of Virgil* (San Francisco: North Point Press, 1983), a reprint of the 1945 edition, published by Pantheon Books. In my text, references to the translation are signaled by Untermeyer, to the Suhrkamp edition by Broch. The secondary literature on Broch's novel is considerable, part of which is listed in the Suhrkamp edition, 521–23. The major secondary literature is well accounted for by Kathleen L. Komar, "The Death of Vergil: Broch's Reading of Vergil's *Aeneid*," *Comparative Literature Studies* 21 (Fall 1984): 255–69. Komar is concerned with Broch's specific uses of the *Aeneid*, relying on Paul Michael Lutzeler's *Materialien zu Hermann Broch's "Der Tod des Vergil"* (Frankfurt am Main: Suhrkamp, 1976). As Komar points out, Lutzeler provides a

list of Broch's quotations from the works of Vergil, with no analysis.
Komar investigates "the underlying suppositions of Broch's interpretation of Vergil's text which shape Broch's own work" (255).
Komar's own demonstration of familiarity with Vergil's text is limited. My essay was a draft when Komar's paper was published. As
suits the character of this book, my purposes are more general. My
essay is set out topically. For a fine linear recapitulation in English of
the novel see Ernestine Schlant, *Hermann Broch* (Boston: Twayne,
1978), 98–117.

   2. Broch in his commentary remarks on the affinity of his book to
a musical structure. His work is analogous to a quartet (Broch 475);
part 1 of the novel goes from andante to maestoso, part 2 is like an
adagio (492).

   3. The principal surviving ancient life is that of the fourth century
A.D. grammarian Aelius Donatus, whose biography is based on a
lost life of Vergil by Suetonius. See *Vitae Vergilianae Antiquae*, ed.
Colin Hardie (Oxford: Clarendon Press, 1966). For the last days and
death of Vergil, see Donatus, sections 35–36. Komar ("*The Death of
Vergil*," 226, n. 1) remarks on how limited Broch's knowledge of the
life of Vergil was, coming only from the *Vita Donati*. Komar echoes
in this concern Theodore Ziolkowski, "Broch's Image of Vergil and
Its Context," *Modern Austrian Literature* 13 (1980): 15–17, who
doubts that Broch ever actually consulted the Latin *vitae*; Ziolkowski contends that Broch used secondary sources that cite the ancient *vitae Vergilianae*. I suggest that the facts given by Donatus are
so brief and yet so well known to humanists that it hardly matters
whether Broch actually read Donatus. We are talking about the
seed, and not necessarily the principal generator of a great modern
novel. See Tenney Frank, "What Do We Know About Vergil?" *Classical Journal* 26 (October 1930–31): 3–11. The Ziolkowski essay was
originally part of the Broch Symposium held at Yale University in
April 1979.

   4. Cf. Doris Stephan, "Thomas Manns *Tod in Venedig* und Hermann Brochs *Vergil*," *Schweizer Monatshefte* 40 (April 1960): 76–83.

5. Cf. Komar, "*The Death of Vergil,*" 260, for the failure of art "to capture the truly significant moment of the living world."

6. See Donatus, 38, for the later poem by one Sulpicius of Carthage that envisions Vergil's deathbed desire to burn the *Aeneid.*

7. Plotia Hieria and Alexis: Donatus, 9, where Alexis is Alexander, cherished by Vergil along with another youth, Cebes. Throughout the novel Broch's Vergil is sexually ambivalent. The passion of Broch's Vergil is to perceive, in the highest Platonic sense, love and beauty.

8. The sentiment of these lines recalls the views of Plato's Aristophanes in the *Symposium.* In this discourse on the nature of love (cf. the references in Chapter 1 on Mann's *Death in Venice*), Plato's Aristophanes conjures up the tale of the creation of the sexes (*Symposium,* 190b–193d), and thereby explains human sexual activity. In Broch's Vergil's delirium, the human being is an object of mockery. An extraordinary modern work is Eugene O'Neill's *Lazarus Laughed,* which depicts the Lazarus of the Gospels, after his resurrection and before his fictional death in Rome, at the court of Tiberius and Caligula. A typical choral song in O'Neill is "Laugh! Laugh! / Fear is no more! / There is no death! / Laugh! Laugh! / There is only life! / There is only laughter!" (New York: Boni and Liveright, 1927), 23.

9. Broch equipped his published novel with a list of the principal quotations from the *Eclogues, Georgics,* and *Aeneid* (Broch 499–500; Untermeyer 492–93). He noted that he had used nearly one hundred citations from Vergil's works. These quotations were derived from the 1799 translation of Vergil's works by Johann Heinrich Voss, with considerable modification by Broch himself (Ziolkowski, "Broch's Image of Vergil," 13–14). I matched the German quotations against the R. A. B. Mynors Oxford Classical Text (1969). They are certainly recognizable. Untermeyer redid the quotations, relying "heavily" on the H. Rushton Fairclough translation in the Loeb Classical Library (Untermeyer 493).

10. A number of Latin poems exist that are in Vergil's style but

are recognized as only pseudo-Vergilian. These poems have been collected as the *Appendix Vergiliana*. The standard Oxford Classical Text of the *AV* (ed. W. V. Clausen et al., 1967) includes the *Aetna*, which also can be read in J. Wight Duff and Arnold M. Duff, eds., *Minor Latin Poets* (New York: Loeb Classical Library, 1961). The Duffs (352–53) take *Aetna* as a composition of the first century A.D., written before the great Campanian earthquake of A.D. 62. The *Aetna*-poet regarded Vesuvius as extinct (431–32). Of course the ruinous earthquake of 62 was followed by the catastrophic eruption of 79.

11. See Ronald Syme, *The Roman Revolution* (Oxford: Clarendon Press, 1939), esp. 322–23, for a brilliant summary of Augustus's unsurpassed position in Rome and his total control of the empire. The critics of Broch naturally emphasize the influence of the times on his novel. See Ziolkowski, "Broch's Image of Vergil," 7–11, both for reference to the totalitarian world of Broch's Europe and to the celebration in 1930 of the bimillennium of Vergil's birth, an influential international observance that brought a slightly faded Vergil back into sharp focus at every level of study. Broch also was guided by Theodor Haecker, *Virgil: Vater des Abendlands* (Leipzig: Hegner, 1931), as pointed out by Ziolkowski ("Broch's Image of Vergil," 9, 11) and Lutzeler (Broch 516). The reader of this book will be interested to know that a recent study of T. S. Eliot gives considerable place to Haecker's book as an influence on Eliot's perception in his well-known essays on Vergil as "an emblematic figure in a convergence of political, social and religious ideas." The author is Gareth E. Reeves, *T. S. Eliot and Vergil* (Ann Arbor, Mich.: University Microfilms, 1981), 102f.

5. Changing Visions

1. This essay was presented in abbreviated form before the Classical Association of the Middle West and South in 1972. The present

version dates from January 1984, when it was delivered as a lecture at Emory University, upon the invitation of the Emory chapter of Eta Sigma Phi, the national classics honor society.

2. Lillian Feder, *Ancient Myth in Modern Poetry* (Princeton, N.J.: Princeton University Press, 1971).

3. Chad Walsh, *Today's Poets: American and British Poetry Since the 1930's* (New York: Charles Scribner's Sons, 1964).

4. T. S. Eliot, *The Complete Poems and Plays, 1909–1950* (New York: Harcourt Brace Jovanovich, 1971), 121.

5. Quoted in Walsh, *Today's Poets,* 73. See also Theodore Roethke, *The Collected Poems* (Garden City, N.Y.: Doubleday, 1966), 200.

6. Walsh, *Today's Poets,* 53. See also William Empson, *Collected Poems* (New York: Harcourt, Brace, 1949), 39.

7. Walsh, *Today's Poets,* 351. See also W. D. Snodgrass, *Heart's Needle* (New York: Alfred A. Knopf, 1959), 17.

8. Eliot, *Complete Poems and Plays,* 117.

9. The point I am making here is to underscore Eliot's departure from specific classical allusion. I still see the outline of the sixth book of Vergil's *Aeneid* as a matrix for the *Four Quartets.* See my "Eliot and Vergil: Parallels in the Sixth Aeneid and *Four Quartets,*" *Vergilius* 12 (1966): 11–20.

10. Northrop Frye, *T. S. Eliot* (Edinburgh and London: Oliver and Boyd, 1963), 67. See also Marjorie Donker, "*The Waste Land* and the *Aeneid,*" *Publications of the Modern Language Association of America* 89 (February 1974): 164–71. For a study of an overall Vergilian presence in Eliot see the Stanford dissertation of Reeves, *T. S. Eliot and Virgil.*

11. Eliot, *Complete Poems and Plays,* 124–25.

12. Ibid, 125.

13. Edmund Wilson, ed., *The Shock of Recognition: The Development of Literature in the United States Recorded by the Men Who Made It* (New York: Farrar, Straus and Cudahy, 1955). The phrase is also in Wilson's epigraph to the book, a quotation from Melville.

14. C. P. Cavafy, *The Complete Poems of Cavafy*, trans. Rae Dalven (New York: Harcourt Brace Jovanovich, 1976), 56.

15. Frederick Nicklaus, *Cut of Noon* (New York: David Lewis, 1971), 14–15.

16. Ibid., 34.

17. Ibid., 30–31.

18. James Dickey, *Drowning with Others* (Middletown, Conn.: Wesleyan University Press, 1962), 47–48.

19. Eliot, *Complete Poems and Plays*, 43–44.

20. Henry James, "Capri and the Bay of Naples," in *The Art of Travel: Scenes and Journeys in America, England, France, and Italy from the Travel Writings of Henry James*, ed. Morton Dauwen Zabel (Garden City, N.Y.: Doubleday, 1958), 424–25.

21. Eliot, *Complete Poems and Plays*, 144.

22. Richard Wilbur, *Things of This World* (New York: Harcourt, Brace, 1956), 43–45.

23. T. S. Eliot, "Tradition and the Individual Talent," in *The Sacred Wood: Essays on Poetry and Criticism* (London: Methuen, 1957), 49.

24. "The Crystal" and "Portrait" are collected in Conrad Aiken, *Sheepfold Hill* (New York: Sagamore Press, 1958), 11–20 and 50.

6. Marguerite Yourcenar

1. An earlier version of this study was presented at Dickinson College on the invitation of the Department of Classics in October 1982. As noted in the prefatory acknowledgements of this book, a revised version was published in *Classical and Modern Literature* 4 (Winter 1984): 87–99. That essay has not been changed, except to add English translations to the quoted French. (*CML* has a policy of no English translations, but this book is for the general reader.) The texts used are as follows: *Feux* (Paris: Gallimard, 1974); *Mémoires d'Hadrien* (Paris: Gallimard, 1974). Page references to these works are given in parentheses. The English translations have been helpful and are the translations used in this study: *Fires*, trans. Dori Katz

(New York: Farrar, Straus, Giroux, 1981), here Katz; *Memoirs of Hadrian*, trans. Grace Frick (1954; reprint, New York: Farrar, Straus, 1963), here Frick. In this study the Anglicized names of the characters are used, except in the quotations from the French and in the chapter titles from *Feux*.

2. For a full description of the Académie Française today and the significance of Yourcenar's election, see Georgia Hooks Shurr, "Marguerite Yourcenar, de l'Académie Française," *Laurels* 52 (Fall 1981): 113–18.

3. For a summary of the sources see David M. Robinson, *Sappho and Her Influence* (New York: Cooper Square, 1963), 39–42.

4. Moses Hadas, "Raison d'être of a Roman Emperor," review of *Memoirs of Hadrian*, by Marguerite Yourcenar, *Saturday Review,* 27 November 1954, 12.

5. Frick, 303. The "Bibliographical Note" in the Frick translation is a slightly expanded version of the "Note" in the original French edition.

6. Herbert W. Benario, *A Commentary on the "Vita Hadriani" in the "Historia Augusta"* (Chico, Calif.: Scholars Press, 1980), p. 13.

7. Ibid., 147–49.

8. Janet Whatley, "*Mémoires d'Hadrien:* A Manual for Princes," *University of Toronto Quarterly* 50 (Winter 1980–81): 235–36.

9. Stewart Perowne, *Hadrian* (London: Hodder and Stoughton, 1960), 181–83. See also Jacques Vier, "L'Empereur Hadrien vu par Marguerite Yourcenar," *Etudes Littéraires* 12 (April 1979): 34. "Cela s'appelait helléniser les Barbares, atticiser Rome, ou, peut-être, immuniser la Ville contre la mort. Du moins la laisserait-il à son fils adoptif, Antonin, en état de survivre aux siècles et même d'affirmer, jusqu'en plein triomphe des vandalismes futurs, une continuité de civilisation à hauteur d'homme." This entire issue was devoted to Marguerite Yourcenar; her appreciation had finally begun.

10. For the observation that Hadrian's world is more accessible to the modern reader than other eras such as Periclean Athens, see

the brief but pithy review of *Hadrien* by John Houston in *Yale French Studies* 27 (Spring–Summer 1961): 140–41.

11. Jean Blot (*Marguerite Yourcenar* [Paris: Seghers, 1980], esp. 131, 123) draws comparisons among several of Yourcenar's fictional characters and Hadrian and sees something of Hamlet in the characterization of the Roman emperor. A recent broad consideration of Yourcenar's work is John Weightman's review of the *Oeuvres romanesques*, "Falling Towards Death," *Times Literary Supplement*, 22 July 1983, 767–68.

12. Mme. Yourcenar died in Maine at the age of eighty-four on 17 December 1987. Her eulogies were world-wide and glowing.

Epilogue

1. See Colin Wilson, *The Outsider* (Boston: Houghton Mifflin, 1956). Wilson discusses characters both real and fictitious in nineteenth- and twentieth-century art and literature.

2. Cf. Paul L. MacKendrick, *The Mute Stones Speak* (New York: St. Martin's Press, 1960), 140–42. Professor MacKendrick directed the summer school of the American Academy in Rome in 1958, of which group the present author was a member.

3. For a warmly informal appreciation of Paul Manship, see Mahonri Sharp Young, "Paul Manship at St. Paul," *Apollo* 122 (September 1985): 228–29.

Bibliography

I. Texts, Plates, and Translations

Aiken, Conrad. *Sheepfold Hill.* New York: Sagamore Press, 1958.

Arnheim, Rudolf. *Picasso's "Guernica": The Genesis of a Painting.* Berkeley and Los Angeles: University of California Press, 1962.

Bell, William S. Introduction and notes to *Gide, "Oedipe"; Cocteau, "La Machine infernale."* New York: Dell, 1968.

Boeck, Wilhelm, and Jaime Sabartés. *Picasso.* New York: Harry N. Abrams, 1955.

Bolliger, Hans. Introduction to *Picasso's "Vollard Suite."* Translated by Norbert Guterman. New York: Harry N. Abrams, 1977.

Broch, Hermann. *The Death of Virgil.* Translated by Jean Starr Untermeyer. 1945. Reprint. San Francisco: North Point Press, 1983.

————. *Der Tod des Vergil: Roman.* Frankfurt am Main: Suhrkamp Verlag, 1976.

Catullus. *C. Valerii Catulli Carmina.* Edited by R. A. B. Mynors. Oxford: Clarendon Press, 1958.

Cavafy, C. P. *The Complete Poems of Cavafy.* Translated by Rae Dalven. New York: Harcourt Brace Jovanovich, 1976.

Cocteau, Jean. *La machine infernale.* Paris: Bernard Grasset, 1934.

————. *Orphée.* Paris: Librairie Stock, 1957.

————. *Orpheus.* Translated by John Savacool. In *The Infernal Machine and Other Plays.* New York: New Directions, 1963.

————. *Orpheus, Oedipus Rex, The Infernal Machine.* Translated, with a foreword and introductory essay, by Carl Wildman. London: Oxford University Press, 1962.

Dickey, James. *Drowning with Others.* Middletown, Conn.: Wesleyan University Press, 1962.

Duncan, David Douglas. *Picasso's Picassos.* New York: Harper and Brothers, 1961.

Eliot, T. S. *The Complete Poems and Plays, 1909–1950*. New York: Harcourt, Brace, Jovanovich, 1971.

Empson, William. *Collected Poems*. New York: Harcourt, Brace, 1949.

Euripides. *The Bacchae*. Translated by William Arrowsmith. In *The Complete Greek Tragedies*, edited by David Grene and Richmond Lattimore. Chicago: University of Chicago Press, 1959.

Gide, André. *Two Legends: Oedipus and Theseus*. Translated by John Russell. New York: Vintage Books, 1958.

Giraudoux, Jean. *La guerre de Troie n'aura pas lieu*. In *Le théatre complet de Jean Giraudoux*. Paris: Ides et Calendes, 1946.

————. *Tiger at the Gates (La Guerre de Troie n'aura pas lieu)*. Translated by Christopher Fry. New York: Oxford University Press, 1955.

Homer. *The Iliad*. Translated by Richmond Lattimore. Chicago: University of Chicago Press, 1961.

Homer. *The Odyssey*. Translated by Richmond Lattimore. New York: Harper and Row, 1967.

Horodisch, Abraham. *Picasso as a Book Artist*. Translated by I. Grafe. New York: World, 1962.

Lieberman, William S. Introduction to *The Sculptor's Studio: Etchings by Picasso*. New York: Museum of Modern Art, 1952.

Mann, Thomas. *Ausgewählte Erzählungen*. Stockholm: Bermann-Fischer Verlag, 1945.

————. *Der Tod in Venedig*. Edited by T. J. Reed. Clarendon German Series. Oxford: Oxford University Press, 1971.

————. *Diaries 1918–1939*. Translated by Richard Winston and Clara Winston. Selection and Foreword by Hermann Kesten. New York: Harry N. Abrams, 1982.

————. *Letters of Thomas Mann, 1889–1955*. Selected and Translated by Richard and Clara Winston, New York: Alfred A. Knopf, 1971.

————. *Stories of Three Decades*. Translated by H. T. Lowe-Porter. New York: Alfred A. Knopf, 1936.

Nicklaus, Frederick. *Cut of Noon*. New York: David Lewis, 1971.

O'Neill, Eugene. *Lazarus Laughed*. New York: Boni and Liveright, 1927.

Plato. *The Collected Dialogues of Plato Including the Letters*. Edited by Edith Hamilton and Huntington Cairns. Bollingen Series. New York: Pantheon, 1961.

Plutarch. *Moralia*. Translated by W. C. Helmbold. Cambridge, Mass.: Loeb Classical Library, 1961.

Rilke, Rainer Maria. *Duino Elegies*. 4th ed. Translated by J. B. Leishman and Stephen Spender, London: Hogarth Press, 1963.

Roethke, Theodore. *The Collected Poems*. Garden City, N.Y.: Doubleday, 1966.

Rubin, William, ed. *Pablo Picasso: A Retrospective*. Chronology by Jane Fluegel. New York: Museum of Modern Art, 1980.

Scriptores Historiae Augustae. Translated by David Magie. Cambridge, Mass.: Loeb Classical Library, 1953.

Snodgrass, W. D. *Heart's Needle*. New York: Alfred A. Knopf, 1959.

Stickney, Trumball. *Poems*. Edited and with an introduction by Amberys R. Whittle. New York: Farrar, Straus and Giroux, 1972.

Vergil. *P. Vergili Maronis Opera*. Edited by R. A. B. Mynors. Oxford: Clarendon Press, 1969.

Vitae Vergilianae Antiquae. Edited by Colin Hardie. Oxford: Clarendon Press, 1966.

Walsh, Chad. *Today's Poets: American and British Poetry Since the 1930's*. New York: Charles Scribner's Sons, 1964.

Wilbur, Richard. *Things of This World*. New York: Harcourt, Brace, 1956.

Williams, Tennessee. *A Streetcar Named Desire*. New York: New Directions, 1947.

Yourcenar, Marguerite. *Feux*. Paris: Gallimard, 1974.

_____. *Fires*. Translated by Dori Katz in collaboration with the author. New York: Farrar, Straus and Giroux, 1981.

_____. *Mémoires d'Hadrien*. Paris: Gallimard, 1974.

_____. *Memoirs of Hadrian*. Translated by Grace Frick in collaboration with the author. 1954. Reprint, New York: Farrar, Straus and Giroux, 1963.

II. Works Cited and Consulted

Agard, Walter Raymond. *Classical Myths in Sculpture*. Madison: University of Wisconsin Press, 1951.

Auerbach, Erich. *Mimesis: The Representation of Reality in Western Literature*. Translated by Willard Trask. Garden City, N.Y.: Doubleday, 1957.

Aylen, Leo. *Greek Tragedy and the Modern World*. London: Methuen, 1964.

Bate, W. Jackson. *The Burden of the Past and the English Poet*. Cambridge, Mass.: Harvard University Press, Belknap Press, 1970.

Benario, Herbert W. *A Commentary on the Vita Hadriani in the Historia Augusta*. Chico, Calif.: Scholars Press, 1980.

Blot, Jean. *Marguerite Yourcenar*. Paris: Seghers, 1980.

Bodkin, Maud. *The Quest for Salvation in an Ancient and a Modern Play*. London: Oxford University Press, 1941.

Brann, Eva. "The Venetian Phaedrus." *College* 24 (July 1972): 1–9.

Brée, Germaine. *Gide*. New Brunswick, N.J.: Rutgers University Press, 1963.

Bullock, Alan. *The Humanist Tradition in the West*. New York: W. W. Norton, 1985.

Bush, Ronald. *T. S. Eliot: A Study in Character and Style*. New York: Oxford University Press, 1983.

Clark, Kenneth. *What Is a Masterpiece?* London: Thames and Hudson, 1979.

Cooper, Douglas. *The Cubist Epoch*. London: Phaidon Press, 1970.

Cooper, Douglas, and Gary Tinterow. *The Essential Cubism: Braque, Picasso and Their Friends, 1907–1920*. London: Tate Gallery, 1983.

Crowson, Lydia. *The Esthetic of Jean Cocteau*. Hanover, N.H.: University Press of New England, 1978.

Donker, Marjorie. "*The Waste Land* and the *Aeneid*." *Publications of the Modern Language Association* 89 (February 1974): 164–71.

Dover, K. J. *Greek Homosexuality*. Cambridge, Mass.: Harvard University Press, 1978.

Durant, Will. *The Life of Greece*. New York: Simon and Schuster, 1939.

Durzak, Manfred. *Hermann Broch: Perspektiven der Forschung*. Munich: Wilhelm Fink Verlag, 1972.

Eliot, T. S. *The Sacred Wood: Essays on Poetry and Criticism*. London: Methuen, 1957.

————. "What Is a Classic?" In *On Poetry and Poets*. New York: Farrar, Straus and Cudahy, 1957.

Evans, Sir Arthur. *The Palace of Minos: A Comparative Account of the Successive Stages of the Early Cretan Civilization as Illustrated by the Discoveries at Knossos*. London: MacMillan, 1921–36. Reprint. New York: Biblo and Tannen, 1964.

Feder, Lillian. *Ancient Myth in Modern Poetry*. Princeton, N.J.: Princeton University Press, 1971.

Fergusson, Francis. *The Idea of a Theater*. Garden City, N.Y.: Doubleday, Anchor Books, 1949.

Fertonani, Roberto. "Echi Classici in *Der Tod in Venedig* di Thomas Mann." *Annali della Facoltà di Lettere e Filosofia dell' Università degli Studi di Milano* 28 (January–August 1975): 17–26.

Four Americans in Paris: The Collections of Gertrude Stein and Her Family. New York: Museum of Modern Art, 1970.

Frank, Tenney. "What Do We Know About Vergil?" *Classical Journal* 26 (October 1930): 3–11.

Frye, Northrop. *T. S. Eliot*. Edinburgh and London: Oliver and Boyd, 1963.

von Gronicka, André. "Myth plus Psychology: A Stylistic Analysis of *Death in Venice*." In *Thomas Mann: A Collection of Critical Essays*, edited by Henry Hatfield. Englewood Cliffs, N.J.: Prentice-Hall, 1964.

Gustafson, Lorraine. "Xenophon and *Der Tod in Venedig*." *Germanic Review* 21 (October 1946): 209–14.

Hadas, Moses. "Raison d'être of a Roman Emperor." Review of

Memoirs of Hadrian, by Marguerite Yourcenar. *Saturday Review,* 27 November 1954.

Haecker, Theodor. *Virgil: Vater des Abendlands.* Leipzig: Hegner, 1931.

Hargrove, Nancy Duvall. *Landscape as Symbol in the Poetry of T. S. Eliot.* Jackson: University Press of Mississippi, 1978.

Haskell, Francis, and Nicholas Penny. *Taste and the Antique: The Lure of Classical Sculpture, 1500–1900.* New Haven, Conn.: Yale University Press, 1981.

Heller, Peter. "Der *Tod in Venedig* und Thomas Manns *Grund-Motiv."* In *Thomas Mann: Ein Kolloquium,* edited by Hans H. Schulte and Gerard Chapple. Bonn: Bouvier Verlag Herbert Grundmann, 1978.

Highet, Gilbert. *The Classical Tradition: Greek and Roman Influences on Western Literature.* New York: Oxford University Press, 1949.

Hirschbach, Frank Donald. *The Arrow and the Lyre: A Study of the Role of Love in the Works of Thomas Mann.* The Hague: Martinus Nijhoff, 1955.

Horwitz, Sylvia L. *The Find of a Lifetime: Sir Arthur Evans and the Discovery of Knossos.* New York: Viking Press, 1981.

Houser, Caroline. *Dionysus and His Circle: Ancient Through Modern.* Cambridge, Mass.: Fogg Art Museum, Harvard University, 1979.

Houston, John. Review of *The Memoirs of Hadrian,* by Marguerite Yourcenar. *Yale French Studies* 27 (Spring–Summer 1961): 140–41.

Hughes, Robert. *The Shock of the New.* New York: Alfred A. Knopf, 1981.

Isemann, Bernd. *Thomas Mann und "Der Tod in Venedig": Eine kritische Abwehr.* Munich: E. W. Bonsels, 1913.

James, Henry. *The Art of Travel: Scenes and Journeys in America, England, France and Italy from the Travel Writings of Henry James.* Edited by Morton Dauwen Zabel. Garden City, N.Y.: Doubleday, 1958.

Jenkyns, Richard. *The Victorians and Ancient Greece*. Cambridge, Mass.: Harvard University Press, 1981.

Kahler, Erich. *The Orbit of Thomas Mann*. Princeton, N.J.: Princeton University Press, 1969.

Komar, Kathleen L. "*The Death of Vergil:* Broch's Reading of Vergil's *Aeneid.*" *Comparative Literature Studies* 21 (Fall 1984): 255–69.

Laine, Amos Lee, and C. Wayne Tucker. "*Death in Venice:* Mann, Britten, and the Greeks." Paper presented at the annual meeting of the Classical Association of the Middle West and South, University of Iowa, April 1977.

Lehnert, Herbert. "Thomas Mann's Early Interest in Myth and Erwin Rohde's *Psyche.*" *Publications of the Modern Language Association* 79 (June 1964): 297–304.

Lemaitre, Georges. *Jean Giraudoux: The Writer and His Work*. New York: Frederick Ungar, 1971.

MacKendrick, Paul L. *The Mute Stones Speak*. New York: St. Martin's Press, 1960.

Massie, Robert K., and Jeffrey Finestone. *The Last Courts of Europe: A Royal Family Album, 1860–1914*. New York: Vendome Press, 1981.

Matthiessen, F. O. *The Achievement of T. S. Eliot: An Essay on the Nature of Poetry*. New York: Oxford University Press, 1959.

Mautner, Franz H. "Die griechischen Anklänge in Thomas Manns *Tod in Venedig.*" In *Wort und Wesen: Kleinere Schriften zur Literatur und Sprache*. Frankfurt: Insel Verlag, 1974.

Murray, Gilbert. *The Classical Tradition in Poetry*. New York: Vintage Books, 1957.

Oates, Whitney J., ed. *From Sophocles to Picasso: The Present-Day Vitality of the Classical Tradition*. Bloomington: Indiana University Press, 1962.

Oxenhandler, Neal. *Scandal and Parade: The Theater of Jean Cocteau*. New Brunswick, N.J.: Rutgers University Press, 1957.

Palau i Febre, Josep. *Picasso: The Early Years, 1881–1907*. New York: Rizzoli, 1981.

Penrose, Roland. *Picasso: His Life and Work*. London: Granada, 1981.

Perowne, Stewart. *Hadrian*. London: Hodder and Stoughton, 1960.

Praz, Mario. *Mnemosyne: The Parallel Between Literature and the Visual Arts*. Bollingen Series, no. 35. Princeton, N.J.: Princeton University Press, 1974.

Raphael, Max. *The Demands of Art*. Translated by Norbert Guterman. Bollingen Series, no. 78. Princeton, N.J.: Princeton University Press, 1968.

Raynal, Maurice. *Picasso*. Translated by James Emmons. Lausanne: Albert Skira, 1953.

Reeves, Gareth E. *T. S. Eliot and Vergil*. Ann Arbor, Mich.: University Microfilms, 1981.

Robinson, David M. *Sappho and Her Influence*. New York: Cooper Square, 1963.

Rogers, Stephen. *Classical Greece and the Poetry of Chénier, Shelley, and Leopardi*. Notre Dame, Ind.: University of Notre Dame Press, 1974.

Rohde, Erwin. *Psyche: The Cult of Souls and Belief in Immortality Among the Greeks*. Translated from the 8th ed. by W. B. Willis. London: Routledge and Kegan Paul, 1950.

————. *Psyche: Seelencult und Unsterblichkeitsglaube der Griechen*. Tübingen: Verlag von J. C. B. Mohr (Paul Siebeck), 1925.

Rowland, Benjamin, Jr. *The Classical Tradition in Western Art*. Cambridge, Mass.: Harvard University Press, 1963.

Rutledge, Harry C. "Classical Latin Poetry: An Art for Our Time." In *The Endless Fountain: Essays on Classical Humanism*, edited by Mark Morford. Columbus: Ohio State University Press, 1972.

————. "Eliot and Vergil: Parallels in the Sixth Aeneid and *Four Quartets*." *Vergilius* 12 (1966): 11–20.

————. "Greece and Rome in the Twentieth Century: Observations on the Classical Tradition and Modernism." *Classical Journal* 78 (December–January 1982–83): 143–49.

————. "Vergil's Dido in Modern Literature." *Classical and Modern Literature* 1 (Summer 1981): 267–73.

Schapiro, Meyer. *Modern Art, Nineteenth and Twentieth Centuries: Selected Papers*. New York: George Braziller, 1978.

Schlant, Ernestine. *Herman Broch*. Boston: Twayne, 1978.

Schmidt, Ernst A. "'Platonismus' und 'Heidentum' in Thomas Manns *Tod in Venedig*." *Antike und Abendland* 20 (1974): 151–78.

Segal, Charles. "Rilke's *Sonnets to Orpheus* and the Orphic Tradition." *Literatur in Wissenschaft und Unterricht* 15 (1982): 367–80.

Shiff, Richard. *Cézanne and the End of Impressionism: A Study of the Theory, Technique, and Critical Evaluation of Modern Art*. Chicago: University of Chicago Press, 1984.

Shurr, Georgia Hooks. "Marguerite Yourcenar, de l'Académie Française." *Laurels* 52 (Fall 1981): 113–18.

Simpson, Malcolm R. *The Novels of Hermann Broch*. Bern: Peter Lang, 1977.

Steegmuller, Francis. *Cocteau: A Biography*. Boston: Little, Brown, 1970.

Steiner, George. *Antigones*. New York: Oxford University Press, 1984.

Stephan, Doris. "Thomas Manns *Tod in Venedig* und Hermann Brochs *Vergil*." *Schweizer Monatshefte* 40 (April 1960): 76–83.

Syme, Ronald. *The Roman Revolution*. Oxford: Clarendon Press, 1939.

Tomlinson, Charles. *Poetry and Metamorphosis*. Cambridge: Cambridge University Press, 1983.

Trustman, Deborah. "France's First Woman 'Immortal.'" *New York Times Magazine*, 18 January 1981, 18–25, 42–44.

Tuchman, Barbara W. *The March of Folly: From Troy to Vietnam*. New York: Alfred A. Knopf, 1984.

Vanggaard, Thorkil. *Phallós: A Symbol and Its History in the Male World*. New York: International Universities Press, 1972.

Vermeule, Cornelius. *European Art and the Classical Past*. Cambridge, Mass.: Harvard University Press, 1964.

Vickery, John B. *The Literary Impact of The Golden Bough*. Princeton, N.J.: Princeton University Press, 1973.

Vier, Jacques. "L'Empereur Hadrien vu par Marguerite Yourcenar." *Etudes Littéraires* 12 (April 1979): 29–35.

Watson-Williams, Helen. *André Gide and the Greek Myth: A Critical Study.* Oxford: Clarendon Press, 1967.

Weightman, John. "Falling Towards Death." Review of *Oeuvres romanesques,* by Marguerite Yourcenar. *Times Literary Supplement,* 22 July 1983, 767–68.

Whatley, Janet. "*Mémoires d'Hadrien:* A Manual for Princes." *University of Toronto Quarterly* 50 (Winter 1980–81): 221–37.

Wilson, Colin. *The Outsider.* Boston: Houghton Mifflin, 1956.

Wilson, Edmund, ed. *The Shock of Recognition: The Development of Literature in the United States Recorded by the Men Who Made It.* New York: Farrar, Straus and Cudahy, 1955.

Winston, Richard. *Thomas Mann: The Making of an Artist, 1875–1911.* New York: Alfred A. Knopf, 1981.

Wood, Michael. *In Search of the Trojan War.* New York: Facts on File Publications, 1985.

Young, Mahonri Sharp. "Paul Manship at St. Paul." *Apollo* 122 (September 1985): 228–29.

Ziolkowski, Theodore. "Broch's Image of Vergil and Its Context." *Modern Austrian Literature* 13 (1980): 1–30.

———. *Hermann Broch.* New York: Columbia University Press, 1964.

Index

Aeschylus, 43, 56, 58–59, 100, 109
Aiken, Conrad, 73, 91–92, 109–10
Anouilh, Jean, 97
Aratus, 77
Aristophanes, Picasso illustrations of *Lysistrata*, 33, 35–36
Art, modern: definitions, 3–4, views of Rilke, 4, Picasso, 37; and the classical tradition, 59, 84–85, 86, 91–92, 120, 121 (n. 5), 125–26 (n. 6), 132 (n. 18)
Athenaeus, 94

"Balloon" (Nicklaus), 81–82
"A Baroque Wall-Fountain in the Villa Sciarra" (Wilbur), 87–88, 89–90, 91
Beauty, cult of, 4, 36–37
Broch, Hermann, 7; *The Death of Vergil*, 63–73, 114
"Burnt Norton" (Eliot), 75, 76

Caesar Augustus, 70–71; in Broch's *The Death of Vergil*, 69–70
Catullus, 85
Cavafy, C. P., "Orophernes," 78, 79
Chaplin, Charles, 94

Chirico, Giorgio de, 60, 101
Clark, Kenneth, 8–9
Cocteau, Jean, 7; *La Machine infernale*, 46–48, 52, 60, 61–62, 94; *Orphée*, 49–51, 52, 62
Cubism, 4, 5, 30–31, 35, 37, 52, 114

Dali, Salvador, 94
Death in Venice (Mann), 10–21, 113–14, 119
The Death of Vergil (Broch), 63–73
Dickey, James, 3; visit to Pompeii, 83; "In the Lupanar at Pompeii," 83–84, 86–87, 90–91
Dietrich, Marlene, 101
"Doctrinal Point" (Empson), 76
Duchamp, Marcel, 52
Duncan, Isadora, 31, 46
Durrell, Lawrence, 78–79

"East Coker" (Eliot), 77
Eliot, T. S., 4, 44, 84, 89, 91, 114–15; "Burnt Norton," 75, 76, 77; "East Coker," 77; *The Family Reunion*, 7, 44, 55–59, 60–61, 77, 114; "Little Gidding," 87

Empson, William, "Doctrinal Point," 76
Epic Cycle (*Cypria*), 52
Euripides, 18–19, 90
Evans, Sir Arthur, 6, 22–23

Fall of Icarus (Picasso), 41–42
"The Far Field" (Roethke), 76
The Family Reunion (Eliot), 55–59, 60–61, 114
Feux (Yourcenar), 93–101
Fry, Christopher. See Giraudoux, Jean

Gide, André, 7, 59; *Oedipe*, 44–46, 60, 62
Giraudoux, Jean, 7; *Amphitryon 38*, 52, 59; *La Guerre de Troie n'aura pas lieu*, 52–55, 62, 94, 114
Guernica (Picasso), 26–29, 38–41, 120

Harmodius and Aristogiton, conspiracy of, 93, 94, 98
Homer, 12, 52, 94; and Yourcenar, 111

"In the Lupanar at Pompeii" (Dickey), 83–84, 86–87, 90–91

James, Henry, 86, 90
Joyce, James, 4, 44

Keats, John, 79

La Guerre de Troie n'aura pas lieu (Giraudoux), 52–55, 62, 94, 114
La Machine infernale (Cocteau), 46–48, 60, 61–62, 94
"Leopardi" (Nicklaus), 80–81, 90
Leopardi, Giacomo, 81, 90
"Little Gidding" (Eliot), 87
Lucretius, 18
Lysistrata (Aristophanes), Picasso's illustrations of, 33, 35–36

Maiuri, Amedeo, 43
Mann, Thomas, 3, 6, 73, 92; *Death in Venice*, 10–21, 113–14, 119
Manship, Paul, *Prometheus*, 119–20
Marie, Queen of Roumania, 46
Mémoires d'Hadrien (Yourcenar), 7–8, 101–11, 119
Metamorphoses (Ovid), Picasso's illustrations of, 32, 35
Millay, Edna St. Vincent, 83
"Minotaur, Horse, and Bird" (Picasso), 38
"Minotaur and Dead Mare Before a Grotto" (Picasso), 38
Minotaur head (Picasso, untitled), 42
Minotauromachy (Picasso), ii, 22, 23–24
Modernism. See Art, modern
Monroe, Marilyn, 59

Mussolini, Benito, 23, 43, 94, 115
"Mythological Scene" (Picasso), 41

Naples, 25, 51, 118; and Frederick Nicklaus, 80–81, 90
Nicklaus, Frederick, 3, 120; European travels, 79; "Balloon," 81–82; "Leopardi," 80–81, 90; "The Pumice Edge," 82–83

Oedipe (Gide), 44–46, 60, 62
O'Neill, Eugene, 6, 59
"The Operation" (Snodgrass), 76
"Orophernes" (Cavafy), 78, 79
Orphée (Cocteau), 49–51, 52, 62
Outsider theme, 113–15, 119–20
Ovid, 16, 77, 119; and Picasso illustrations, 32, 35

Parthenon, 1, 30, 31, 79
Picasso, Pablo, 4, 5, 21–42, 114; Fall of Icarus, 41–42; Guernica, 26–29, 38–41, 120; Lysistrata illustrations, 33, 35–36; Metamorphoses illustrations, 32, 35; "Minotaur, Horse, and Bird," 38; "Minotaur and Dead Mare Before a Grotto," 38; Minotaur head (untitled), 42;

Minotauromachy, ii, 22, 23–24; "Mythological Scene," 41; The Pipes of Pan, 31; Rape of the Sabines, 41; "Satyr and Sleeping Woman" ("Faun Unveiling a Sleeping Woman"), 25, 34; Satyr, Faun, Centaur, 42; Still Life with Red Bull's Head, 34, 42; Studio with Plaster Head, 31, 116; Suite Vollard, 24–25, 30–31; Three Musicians, 31; Three Women at the Spring, 31, 117; Woman in White, 31; Women Running on the Beach, 31
The Pipes of Pan (Picasso), 31
Plato, 87; Phaedrus, 12, 14; Symposium, 12–14, 15, 17
Pompeii, 25, 118; and James Dickey, 83–84, 86–87
Prometheus (Rockefeller Center), 119–20
"The Pumice Edge" (Nicklaus), 82–83

Rape of the Sabines (Picasso), 41
Rembrandt, 40
Renault, Mary, 6
Rilke, Rainer Maria, 4
Roethke, Theodore, "The Far Field," 76
Rome, 25, 74–75, 115, 118; and Frederick Nicklaus, 81–82, 120; and Richard Wilbur, 88, 120

"Satyr and Sleeping Woman"
("Faun Unveiling a Sleeping
Woman") (Picasso), 25, 34
Satyr, Faun, Centaur (Picasso),
42
Sebastian, Saint, 17
Snodgrass, W. D., "The Opera-
tion," 76
Socrates, 99
Sophocles, 43, 94
Stein, Gertrude, 74
Stickney, Trumbull, 1, 3
Still Life with Red Bull's Head
(Picasso), 34, 42
Studio with Plaster Head
(Picasso), 31, 116
Styron, William, 75
Suite Vollard (Picasso), 24–25,
30–31
Surrealism, 4, 7, 24, 48, 52,
59–60, 99
Syme, Sir Ronald, 7, 70

Three Musicians (Picasso), 31
Three Women at the Spring
(Picasso), 31, 117

Thucydides, 18, 98
Tiger at the Gates (Giraudoux),
52–55, 62, 94, 114

Vergil, 50, 51, 60, 77, 85–86, 87,
90, 109; in Broch's *The Death
of Vergil*, 63–73, 114
Versailles Treaty, 23, 52
Virgil. *See* Vergil

Wilbur, Richard: fellow of the
American Academy in Rome,
88; "A Baroque Wall-Fountain
in the Villa Sciarra," 87–88,
89–90, 91
Williams, Tennessee, 1, 3, 59,
74–75
Woman in White (Picasso), 31
Women Running on the Beach
(Picasso), 31
Woolf, Virginia, 74
World War II, 43, 52–53, 62, 74

Yourcenar, Marguerite, 7–8;
Feux, 93–101; *Mémoires
d'Hadrien*, 7–8, 101–11, 119